Mechademia : Second Arc

Mechademia: Second Arc (ISSN 1934-2489) is published twice a year in the spring and fall by the University of Minnesota Press, 111 Third Avenue South, Suite 290, Minneapolis, MN 55401-2520. http://www.upress.umn.edu

Postmaster: Send address changes to *Mechademia: Second Arc*, University of Minnesota Press, 111 Third Avenue South, Suite 290, Minneapolis, MN 55401-2520.

All submissions must be between 5000–6000 words. Essays that are substantially longer cannot be accepted. Citations should be given in *Chicago Style* 17th ed. using bibliographic endnotes rather than footnotes or in-text citations. Please see the Mechademia Style Guide (see PDF on mechademia.net) for more details on citation style and essay formatting. Submissions and editorial queries should be sent to submissions@mechademia.net.

Books for review should be addressed to

Forrest Greenwood
Indiana University Innovation Center
2719 E 10th St
Bloomington, IN 47408

Brian White
#101 Etosu O2, 26-14
Edogawa-ku, Shinozaki-machi 4-chome
Tokyo
Japan

Address subscription orders, changes of address, and business correspondence (including requests for permission and advertising orders) to *Mechademia: Second Arc*, University of Minnesota Press, 111 Third Avenue South, Suite 290, Minneapolis, MN 55401-2520.

Subscriptions: Regular rates, U.S.: individual, 1 year, $21.50; libraries, 1 year, $81. Outside the U.S. add $5 for each year's subscription. Checks should be made payable to the University of Minnesota Press. Back issues are $21.50 for individuals, $21.50 for libraries (plus $6 shipping for the first copy, $1.25 for each additional copy inside the U.S.; $9.50 shipping for the first copy, $6 for each additional copy, outside the U.S.). *Mechademia: Second Arc* is available online through the JSTOR Current Scholarship Program at http://jstor.org/r/umnpress.

....

Mechademia : Second Arc

VOLUME 12, NO. 2
SPRING 2020

ASIAN MATERIALITIES

· · · Introduction

The initial idea for this issue of *Mechademia* was to explore how attending to materiality (and medium) would reveal the transnationality of media in/across/from Asia. While the works in this issue do not explicitly take on more radical approaches to materiality (like that of Jane Bennett's "vibrant matter"), material is by no means seen as inert. Rather, it is considered as active (or at the very least resilient), producing interactions with consequences that have important implications should one follow their chain of effects. The articles in this issue utilize this point of departure either to engage with how certain cultural objects enact and enable some actions or viewpoints or to explore formal approaches to examining those objects and their dynamics.

It is also worth noting the emphasis on conventionality in conjunction with the material in the articles that follow. Many of the works examined here are part of "popular cultures" that embrace the often-derided repetitious practice of conventionality. In the context of considering materiality, there is a much longer tradition in the examination of the "high arts" to valorize those specific works that bring our attention to the dynamics of human and material. In such instances, these art works are praised for their uniqueness, as they actively raise our understanding of these interactions in a manner strikingly different than other works of a similar type. In other words, the stand out examples of "art" are made to stand out due to their distance from common conventions as employed in works of that type. Thinking through the inverse of this, we might wonder not just about the specificity of these stand out works but how other more conventional objects hide (or display in ways we have not yet discovered) their materiality. Thus, we might think of material in correspondence with convention, as the conventional must always be worked through the material, where the two inform one another. In this sense, materiality is taken to also include repeated material practices. This may initially seem out of step with trending conceptions of materiality. However, the development of recent transmedial approaches have brought into focus the striking resemblance of the myriad objects in the media mix, each object born of very different materials and technologies, inviting us to realize the overlap of conventions as it simultaneously calls attention to the variety of materials and mediums involved.

1

This is important to consider as anime, manga, and games studies have, after many years, become increasingly recognized as specific fields of research, and we can now contribute back to the fields we sprung from through our own innovations. In a sense, media specifics such as materiality and conventions, along with the interactions between those media, are what separate our objects of study from those of other disciplines; it is their exploration that is precisely what we have to offer, especially to fields like media studies. But this specificity is also highly associated with particular spatial and cultural coordinates. Notably, in the study of anime, manga, and games, we have to contend with certain geographical elements, whether implicitly or explicitly. For instance, anime and manga (and some types of games) are very deeply associated with Japan, yet we find their production, distribution, and consumption across the globe and, in particular, across Asia. We thus have to consider the local particularities and institutionalized disciplinary structures that bring our study of these media into contact with the methodologies of area studies, in this case Japan studies, and more prominently Asian studies, in general.

With this in mind, it is also worth pointing out that this issue by no means intends to represent all of Asia (nor could it possibly be expected to do so). However, there is a marked focus not only on East Asia but most conspicuously on Japan. This was not the intention of the editors but an organic outcome from the submissions, which were heavily weighted toward Japan. There was an earnest effort made to be as inclusive of other areas of Asia as possible, but part of the process of editing a journal is to work within the bounds of the materials received and the topic at hand. I raise this point here not just to acknowledge the lack of representation of works on other parts of Asia, to show that it is erroneous to equate East Asia with "Asia" (wherever those boundaries are drawn). In addition, I want to highlight this emphasis on Japan because it underscores a deeper dynamic at play here, not just of the dominance of the nation in the discourse on the objects of study but how Japan itself operates in relation to the rest of Asia, in particular in regard to certain forms of popular culture. This is a topic revealed throughout the articles featured here.

Focusing on the divisiveness of Japanese media in South Korea, Chloé Paberz opens this issue with her ethnographic study of illustrators in Seoul and their relationship to Japanese manga. Paberz details certain conceptions of illustration styles, industry practices, and cross-border dynamics of South Korean illustrators and how they relate to what is seen as Japanese manga.

In their own accounts, these illustrators feel marginalized and display an overt effort to distance themselves from local regimes of cultural production, seeing a capacity for liberation through their acquiring of the technical skills of drawing, in particular through the style of so-called Japanese manga. What arises is thus a conception of a community of craftsmen, where mastery of skills is acknowledged as a bodily education, one that embraces copying (while still acknowledging particularity) and does not have the same boundaries as the nation-state.

The reconciliations and tensions between copying and a particular touch, of hierarchies and communities that extend beyond national borders that Paberz reveals, are taken up in various forms throughout the articles of this issue. For instance, the close association of Japan with anime and its effect on a type of transnationality is explored in the article by Stevie Suan through an engagement with anime's media-form (the interplay among material, medium, and convention). Examining the visuality of the animation, character acting, and transnational production networks, anime's media-form is seen as a performance embodying a tension between the particular location of its execution and its relation to other instantiations. As such, contrary to a concrete grounding as Japanese, anime performance enacts a spatiality that is constituted through a connection to other locales, encapsulating the frictions of globalization: located in one place but related to others, beyond the bounds of the modernistic spatiality of the nation-state. By examining this spatiality in relation to the openly transnational anime *Shikioriori* about locales in China, Suan explores how even place-focused anime enact the problematics of this dislocation, apparently situated in a particular location yet also displaced elsewhere.

Moving from performance to play, the next article, by Selen Çalık Bedir, examines how material specifics (and subsequently, medium specifics) enable a type of "(re)playing" anime. Concerned with the dynamics of limited animation in particular, the combination of stillness and sounds produces a field of ambiguity even in a media-form so riddled with conventionality, keeping us somehow withheld from accurately predicting what will happened next. Developed through an analysis of the gamelike in anime, Çalık Bedir relates this play of prediction and unpredictability to the larger crisis of causality in our information-saturated society, where it seems as if everything can easily be foreseen. Çalık Bedir pulls at the distinctions between mediums and details how anime overcome the limits of the storyworld through the weakening of causal links to allow for alternative possibilities.

Continuing the concern with medium specifics, Lukas R. A. Wilde's article focuses on the symbology of manga, drawing on theories of semiotics and narratology and putting them in dialogue with the ideas of manga theorist Natsume Fusanosuke. Relating to the focus on convention and the importance of material in its execution, Lukas notes not only how the symbols employed in manga are part of a larger cultural circulation of images but also that we can never be too sure of the validity of represented objects to their corresponding storyworld. Wilde explores this through distinctive thresholds for manga, explicating a distinction between manga's modality and mediality, how despite seeing similar symbols in signages (for example, in subways and parks in Japan) they are read quite differently when printed as manga. Lukas thus provides a foundation for opening up the range of possibilities for both the disconnect from and relation to representations afforded by manga.

In the next article, Jaqueline Berndt conducts a focused reading of the *In This Corner of the World* manga in relation to the animated film, exploring the material specifics of the media while taking into account the impact of industrial genres within Japan. Berndt explicates the marginality of the manga on multiple registers: in the shift gained from reading in the margins, to the marginality of the manga in terms of genre, and the view from the margins of Japanese narratives of World War II. Read through the intimate intricacies of the line work, Berndt's article provides careful attention to form without giving in to lofty notions of freedom from context. In her reading, Berndt reveals a certain degree of criticality, bypassing an overindulgence of authorial intent, showing how mangaesque conventions and the materiality of publication afford a more distributive sense of agency on the part of the author/artist, involving the reader, and drawing us into the conjoining of past and present.

Dalma Kálovics follows with a detailing of the complex interaction between material formats of publication and the formal dynamics of manga. Kálovics reveals the clash of medium, media, and the transnational for contemporary manga in Japan as the industry moves toward digitalization, with heavy pressure from the popular webtoon platforms and products, largely from South Korea. She juxtaposes this present-day problem to the issues of format that occurred with shôjo manga in the 1960s (a woefully understudied era) to show how there were similar issues about organization, standardization, paneling, and sizing that are currently encountered with manga moving from paper/print to the internet/software application.

Akiko Sugawa-Shimada's article returns us to the issue of space and the examination of 2.5-D culture. Sugawa-Shimada reveals how this new cultural phenomenon—a hot topic of discussion in Japan—builds from the material-rich environment of the media mix and the internet. However, in its theatrical forms, 2.5-D cultural practice places emphasis on the live, the playful blurring of boundaries between real actor and fictional character and the integral engagement of fans. Developing a conception of what she calls "communities of preferences," Sugawa-Shimada explores the potential of the transnational communities that these 2.5-D fan interactions can foster through an analysis of testimonies from Chinese fans. With 2.5-D productions now regularly occurring across Asia, Sugawa-Shimada sets up the exploration of these cultural practices beyond Japan.

The final article, by Edmond Ernest dit Alban continues the exploration of the circulation of commodities and the constitution of space via the interactivity of fans. Through the example of the prominent Boys' Love–fandom mecca of Otome Road in Ikebukuro, Tokyo, Ernest dit Alban examines the synergies and frictions produced by pedestrians, shop owners, and the exchange of certain types of products. He retraces the history of this engagement that, over time, physically changed the urban area, drawing our attention to the constitution of place through the material, the physical, and the aesthetic in motion. Building from the theories of anime, manga, and games, whereby there is a remixing and reusing of images, a complex interaction between the exercise of agency by the fandom and the involvement of industry coincide on and through the shifting terrain. Ernest dit Alban's analysis reveals both mobility and situatedness, echoing the conclusions of many of the authors throughout this issue, highlighting how materiality seems to both locate us and expose the intensity of movements occurring.

Stevie Suan

Communities of Craftsmen

Reflections on Japanese Manga from
South Korean Manhwaga

CHLOÉ PABERZ

In the last few years, several South Korean illustrators have been publishing successful comics inside and outside of Korea. These comics are called *manhwa* in Korean, which shares the same etymology as the Japanese term *manga* and the Chinese term *manhua*; the term is based on identical sinograms and only differs in pronunciation.[1] While manhua/manhwa/manga tend to refer to comics in general, there seems to be a consensus on the fact that manga differs from American and European comics. The recent rise of Korean and Chinese comics has brought up some confusion around the classification of such works: should they fall under the manga category, as is generally the case for the international market or, as seen in some French libraries, should manhwa be literally put on a different shelf than manga? Since Korea has also developed original narrativities based on the possibilities of reading online comics (webtoon) on smartphones, should webtoons be considered as the sole flagships of Korean comics?

In South Korea, the classification of manhwa as manga has been perceived as a problem to Korean cultural promotion agencies. In general, any confusion between Korean and Japanese things raises great tension in the peninsula, largely associated with the collective trauma caused by the colonization of Korea by Japan. Although South Korean culture is widely recognized today, for a long time people and institutions were worried (and some of them still are) that the rest of the world will mistake Korean with Japanese or Chinese culture. This general frame explains why, in the last decade, the cultural promotion agencies have been reluctant to use the label "manga," and why they have tended to emphasize Korean manhwa's specificities in an effort to characterize a Korean identity to the media. By refusing to use the Japanese "manga," the promotion agencies want to prove that Korea can create its own art, and that Korean artists are truly innovative and not mere copycats of Japanese artists. This proof of creativity is a matter of politics as well as a matter of economics.

However, in order to connect this general frame with more concrete, down-to-earth, daily practices and views in Korean society, this article takes a step back from these large-scale nationalist concerns by exploring ethnographic data collected at a smaller scale. Between 2009 and 2010, I conducted ethnographic research in a South Korean game company for ten months. I performed interviews and participant observation while doing small tasks for the company, sharing in the life of this company by following the employees during their working days, evenings, dinners, trips to game conventions and various events. Borrowing the methodology developed by French anthropologists such as Sophie Houdart[2] and Emmanuel Grimaud,[3] this research offers a detailed account of the creation process by focusing on details, material issues, minor dramas, and small victories that characterize the activity of collective creation practices and that eventually disappear in the type of accounts that focus more on structures or results.

I have drawn on this ethnography in order to understand how Korean illustrators use the reference to Japanese manga in their everyday life. Do they reject or avoid it, as institutions tend to do? What is the actual role of the reference to Japan in their work practice? The first part of this article is dedicated to the Korean illustrators' discourses regarding Japanese manga, and the second part explores how reference to Japanese elements (media, language) is a part of a larger reference frame that shapes the material organization (objects, gestures) of their everyday activities.

Is the Game Industry a Japanese-Friendly Environment?

When I first went to South Korea in 2005, I was surprised by the frequency, the variety, and the vehemence of Korean criticism toward Japan and Japanese people. Criticisms ranged from accusations related to historical facts or political issues (thefts of national treasures, lack of compensation for war crimes, the territorial ownership of the Liancourt Rocks, to cite a few) to perceptions of ugliness or beliefs in inherited immorality, and sometimes even imagining links between these issues and natural disasters. Such violent anti-Japanese discourses, while not dominant, can still be heard in contemporary Korea and sometimes surface on social networks today.

In contradistinction to this, when the game company accepted my presence as an ethnographer, one of the first things that I noticed was that many people there spoke Japanese and openly expressed their love for Japanese culture. The place seemed exempt of the tension that usually arises when Japan was mentioned in other contexts. Many desks were decorated with figurines from Japanese manga and anime such as *OnePiece* or *Gundam*, especially in the area where the graphics team worked. One third of the employees spoke Japanese; some of them had learned it in school, while others had learned by themselves through games, pop music, TV shows, online communities, or manga. When I expressed my admiration for their language skills, they generally refused to take credit for it, pretending that it was easy for them because of the numerous similarities between the Japanese and the Korean language. While this answer might be interpreted as an expression of basic politeness in Korean, it tends to minimize the fact that their fluency was the result of a genuine interest in Japanese culture and a serious commitment to learning the language.

Since the high ratio of Japanese speakers in this workplace seemed unusual, I decided to compare how many people spoke Japanese in each team. The company's CEO had told me that he was interested in foreign languages and was learning English. I had also heard several times that speaking Japanese was a considerable asset in the game business. I started my survey with this CEO, while we were having lunch with his assistant, and asked him if he spoke Japanese. He stopped eating, put down his spoon on the table, raised one eyebrow and answered: "Do I look like a Japanese person to you?" This was a reminder of the tension mentioned before, as well as a hint toward the distinctive features of the Japanese-speaking community.

At the end of my survey, it turned out that almost no one from the marketing or programming teams spoke Japanese. Most of the Japanese speakers belonged to the *geuraepik tim* ("graphics team"), which was a well-known fact in the company. Not only did everyone in the company know that speaking Japanese was common for the illustrators but the ones who did not speak Japanese considered themselves to be an exception. According to them, most of their fellow manhwaga spoke Japanese. Their depiction of a majority of Japanese-speaking illustrators was partly exaggerated, but it indicated a norm shared by the graphics team and other teams alike. This norm was part of a positive attitude toward Japan that was neither general nor abstract but rooted in the personal stories that I collected during interviews. In the account detailed below, we will see how comics, and especially Japanese comics, played a pivotal role in the germination of their professional vocation.

"Nothing but Scribble": Professional Vocations

Before I go any further, I would like to note that I mainly use the word "manhwaga" as a generic term to refer to the illustrators interviewed for this research. However, for my interviewees, "manhwaga" usually referred to accomplished comic artists. This terminological choice aims at including every person who is involved in the creation of the visual elements of manhwa-related industries (manhwa, animation, games, and affiliated products) and whose main professional skill is drawing. I have translated this term as "illustrators," even if my interviewees tended to use the Korean equivalent of "illustrator," *saphwaga* or *illeoseuteureiteo*, only for specific positions such as children's book illustration. I should also mention that in Korean, "manhwa" does not necessarily imply a Korean origin (one can talk of a Japanese manhwa or an American manhwa). It is not limited to humoristic comic strips, and can refer to printed, animated, or online products. In the game company, the most inclusive term was *geuraepik* (from the English "graphic"), and all its derivatives *(geuraepik tim, geuraepik dijain, geuraepik ateu)*. Members of the graphics team had the name of the team written on their business cards rather than their specific positions. The English term "graphic designer" was also used *(geuraepik dijaineo)* not as a generic word but as one of the many positions inside the company. Rather than use a generic term, the members of the team and their colleagues from other teams tended to use specific titles related to the tasks that they were temporarily allocated, such as animation *(aenimeisyeon)*, character design *(kaerikteo dijain)*, background work *(baegyeong jageop)*, and so on. Considering the lack of a generic term that could include all the members of the team, and the fact that almost all of them aspired to ultimately attain the position of manhwaga, I use this term as a general category that could include accomplished manhwaga, aspiring manhwaga, and part-time manhwaga. The following pages will hopefully shed light on these vocabulary issues.

To focus my findings, I mainly use extracts from two semi-directive interviews with two illustrators, Su-min and Kyung-han. Su-min is one of the founding members of the company and designed the images for the game prototype, before the company hired an art director who adapted the original style. Su-min is a friendly and relaxed man in his early thirties, and one of the people who spends the longest hours at work. He is involved in almost all the important decisions made by the company and in charge of various parts of the graphic team, mainly designing full-screen images for the game and full-page images for the printed material that goes with the game. I asked Su-min how he became a graphic designer, he replied:

> I used to draw all the time when I was a kid. In class, I would do nothing but scribble on my notebooks. At home, I would spend my time copying the manhwa that I owned. I also watched a lot of anime. While growing up, I started to think that maybe I could make a living out of it: combine pictures and stories. To me, both are equally important and both must be of high quality. The pictures have to be beautiful, and the stories have to be fun, like in Urasawa Naoki's manga. . . . I went to university for a short period, but I was unable to get my degree because my family did not have enough money to pay for tuition. In college, I studied animation: it was fascinating! I have always loved animation, because of Japanese manga and anime. More importantly, it was a way for me to express myself. But in the end, here I am, making videogames.

The second illustrator is Kyung-han, who arrived at the company more recently. He is a few years younger than Su-min, visibly more serious and more introverted than his colleagues, who often teased him for being unreasonably invested in his passions. I also asked him how he became a graphic designer:

KH: "I have been drawing since I was a little kid. Back then I did not think that it could be my job one day. This idea came to me in high school. I started to think about it more seriously, and I enrolled in design studies. Design was the closest thing to what I wanted to do. Competition is too fierce to enter art schools. I changed majors when I decided to work in the game industry. But now I want to change again, and I want to do manhwa. I would like to create a perfect manhwa, both in drawing style and contents. Until this day, I have never found a single manhwa that satisfies both criteria.

C: What about in games?

KH: It's not even worth mentioning! The drawings are pathetic!

C: What do you mean?

KH: Let me explain. When I eat, I hold my chopsticks like this, you see? My hand is a bit tilted; my wrist is like this; my whole body adjusts to the presence of the chopsticks. Our bodies are made of muscles, right? Everything is connected, so it's not nonsense: there is a correct way to depict movement. But in games, when characters are eating, their posture is totally unnatural.

[He starts miming the unnatural postures, which makes me laugh.]

KH: I am not kidding! You can check it yourself next time; take almost any game: you'll see, the postures are rubbish."

These extracts reveal several narrative patterns that can also be found in most of the interviews with this team's members. These common patterns include a narrative in three steps: first, a (relatively marginalizing) passion for drawing, developed during early childhood in a poor but supportive family; second, the transformation of this passion into a professional vocation associated with an attempt to improve through specialized education; third, a disillusion caused by working in the game industry. Each step involves a transformation of the status of drawing. In the first stage, drawing is depicted as a natural inclination of a body to "scribble." Then, drawing becomes a savoir faire requiring an advanced education and embedded in a professional project. In its last stage, drawing is depicted as a skill wasted in (or endangered by) a mediocre environment.

This narrative indicates that drawing comics is considered a profession, and that this professional activity can either be properly carried out in the comics and anime industries or considered a fallback solution in the video game industry, where it is easier to find employment. While programmers and game designers often referred to video games in their interview as inspiration sources for their work, illustrators mentioned manga and anime rather than games as inspiration. Working in the game industry was perceived as being very different from working in the manhwa industry. My interviewees often hoped that this fallback solution was only temporary. They were holding on to their dream of becoming manhwa artists someday and creating a combination of good pictures and good stories. They were also aware of the fact that most game companies had very short lifespans, which could also play a role in this representation of game work as a temporary activity.

Korean Manhwa Versus Japanese Manga

This sense of the aesthetic superiority of comics over videogames was associated with another comparison between comics from Korea and comics from Japan. When I asked Kyung-han for advice on Korean manhwa, he answered with the following:

KH: "Don't even bother reading Korean manhwa. They are garbage compared to Japanese manga. They have no value. You would only ruin your eyes.

C: Really?

KH: Well, what I mean is not that Korean manhwa are all bad. . . . But . . . considering that Japan has a longer history of creating comics, it is only normal that they have better ones. Do you remember what I told you about the postures? Well that's exactly the kind of things that you will find in Korean comics. When it comes to comics, Korea is only following (*ttara-hada*) Japan."

Kyung-han expressed his opinions in a direct way, but his colleagues also tended to praise Japanese comics and did not show much enthusiasm about Korean comics. Even if Kyung-han's answer surprised me by its radicality, he immediately followed by bringing in a historical explanation. His reaction shows that even if he could not think of any respectable Korean comic (which was not the case for everyone: several employees mentioned *Dooly the Little Dinosaur [Agigongnyong dulli]* with tenderness[4]), one could not explain it by a natural incapacity but rather to a logical aftermath of history. This idea is relatively common in South Korea and abroad, including in academic works that tend to focus on the influence of Japanese manga on Korean manhwa rather than on how they influence each other.[5]

This narrative was a common view among manhwaga, especially because most of them were born in the 1970s and 1980s and had vivid memories of this era. They all insisted on the idea that they had witnessed radical and extremely fast changes in Korean society since their childhoods. These changes touched upon various aspects of everyday life and society, including leisure activities. Hyun-woo, another member of the graphic team, brought this to my attention while evoking the first comics he had read as a child:

It was . . . my father who gave me my first comic. In the 1980s, Japanese manga were forbidden in our country, because of the protectorate. It was possible for us to find a few manga that were imported illegally, but there was almost nothing. What was possible to find, though, was copies. We were kids and thought those comics were Korean! The copyists would change the names of the characters and change parts of the scenery that could have been identified as Japanese.

Here, Hyun-woo refers to a protectorate that was supposed to save Korea from "cultural invasion" from Japan. This protectorate existed officially until 2001, but imports were tolerated since 1998. It was a very important measure considering that during the Japanese colonial period, Korean people *were* deprived of their culture. Prohibition laws changed several times under the colonial administration: Koreans were forbidden to publish books in their own language, or even to speak Korean. This led to political movements aimed at safeguarding Korean culture and raised deep and lasting anxieties in the general population regarding the possible disappearance of Korean culture and its replacement by Japanese culture.

This historical narrative passes as common knowledge among Koreans, but the legal situation regarding Japanese products might have been more complicated, with some imports being officially legal in the early 1990s and several readers probably being aware of the Japanese origin of these comics.[6] Nevertheless, their circulation was not as free as in Western countries or as in contemporary Korea. The narrative of prohibition would also be in line with the "narrative of the misfit" at the core of their professional culture.[7] If reading Japanese comics was illegal, the readers were already engaged in a counterculture opposed to the legal system. This could be part of a playful attitude that was shared in the workplace and consisted of depicting oneself as "strange," "otaku," or "marginal," which echoes the depiction of Japan as a nonconformist, individualistic, skilled, creative and "strange country" (*isanghan nara*). Such a conception of Japan might be familiar to contemporary readers, but it contrasts with older writings by Westerners and Japanese intellectuals alike who described Japan as "an imitating country."[8] My interviewees explicitly associated Japan with an idea of freedom and excellence, as opposed to their own country. The reference to Japan could thus be understood as a way to take some distance from Korean mainstream culture. Japan, however, was not the only reference and, more broadly, this company's employees seemed very open-minded about foreign models and kept building comparisons between Korea and other countries.

While there is a general and vivid tension in Korea around the idea of foreign influences, the illustrators did not seem to share this anxiety. In the second part of this article, I suggest that they associated different values to the idea of influence, and even to the idea of copying.

Copying and Creating

Illustrators' attitudes toward copying seemed highly ambivalent. When I asked Su-min and Kyung-han if there were parts of their work that they disliked, they answered as follows:

> I really hated all these long hours copying the game contents, this mandatory training. . . . I was bored to death! But it's unavoidable, in order to keep a coherent visual identity for the game. (Su-min)

> It took me a very long time to adapt to the style of the game. This is because this style is very different from the character design that I was using at my previous job. It took me about three months, I think. For three months, I was training all the time, copying the existing graphic designs. It's super annoying, but it's the only way. (Kyung-han)

This type of complaint was actually very common among illustrators employed at the game company. Nobody seemed to enjoy this period of copying, but everybody agreed on its necessity. Copying is seen as a means of acquiring a skill: here, the skill consists in being able to reproduce the graphical style chosen for a game and applied by all members of the graphics team. Since I explicitly asked the question, the illustrators complained about it because it is time-consuming and dull, but they unanimously agreed on the fact that it is a constitutive and necessary part of the collective creative process. Copying thus belongs to a category of learning processes called *frayage* in French:[9] it indicates the repetition of a gesture until it becomes automatic, strictly identical from one performance to the other, and perfectly mastered in order to produce exactly the intended effect.

Drawing as a "Technique of the Body"[10]

The members of the graphics team also believed that, in general, copying was necessary in order to learn how to draw. In one of the interviews, a member of the team stated: "If you want to *become a good manhwaga*, there is nothing to learn. You just have to *look* at how other people do, and then do it yourself." Many of his colleagues expressed similar views: for them, copy was the only way to improve as a comic artist. As with the language abilities mentioned earlier, such an answer might fall under the implicit rules of Korean politeness by minimizing one's merit in being skilled. However, in addition to cultural speech habits, it also reveals a strong belief in the (virtually unlimited) potential of the body. The vast majority of my interviewees claimed that they were not good at school and insisted on their lack of formal education in art (most of them did not receive any). Drawing was not valued in the curriculum: their skill was thus excluded from the standards of school, which again conveys the idea of marginality mentioned earlier. Drawing skills were considered as neither intellectual aptitude nor natural talent but rooted in the body as a result of a patient education of the body. They also considered that this long education gave them no particular merit and declared that, as children, they would copy their favorite manhwa and manga just for fun. The tremendous amount of time spent drawing was minimized and not quantified: the patient incorporation of this bodily skill was thus made relatively invisible and its mechanisms remained opaque. Reduced to "nothing," these skills were resistant to any form of elucidation or valuation. Those techniques of the body were also considered as personal and nonstandard: in order to achieve the same graphical result, every member of the graphic team followed his own ways regarding the rhythm and type of gestures, the observation materials, the type of paper, the posture of the body, and so on. This built an intimate connection between the illustrators and what they were drawing, that they were often reluctant to abandon when the managers made decisions on what would be kept and what would be rejected.

What graphic designers did not like about copying the game visuals was not the copy itself but the fact that they were learning a style that was only temporary and not useful for them in the long term. They could use it only while designing this specific game and would have to abandon it as soon as they would begin to work on another project. As Kyung-han put it, their "hand did not belong to them, it belongs to the artistic director"; one of his colleagues said that she was afraid of losing her drawing skills if she continued using only this style for too long. However, copying masterpieces (from Korean manhwaga, Japanese mangaka, or any respected illustrator from another country) was a shared enjoyable experience and a central part of the patient education of the body required to "become a manhwaga." Copying thus appears simultaneously as a dangerous burden and as a (if not the only) work tool.

Secret Sketchbooks

The last part of the article focuses on how these manhwaga overcome the frustrations of their position and how they pursue their dream of becoming skilled artists. The illustrators in this company were very critical of their job, but they still loved their activity: drawing. When I asked Kyung-han what was his favorite thing about working here, he cast a look around and pulled a big sketchbook from under his desk. There were several sketchbooks there, filled with original characters that he had been drawing during lunch breaks and down times. He commented:

> Because of my work here, I don't have enough time to train. What I really want to work on is my personal projects. You see, this is my style. It has nothing in common with the game. This is what I like, drawing this type of characters. This is my taste.
>
> It is very hard to become a proper comic artist. If I want to get a chance, I need to train hard. That's why I spend every free moment of my time drawing, to improve my technique.

The colleague sitting next to him also had a similar space for his personal works. The managers were well aware of the secret sketchbooks. They turned a blind eye to it, as long as the manhwaga finished their paid work on time. This practice is not uncommon in game companies in Korea or elsewhere; it is more or less expected and sometimes even encouraged by the companies. For example, at Linden Lab, anthropologist Thomas Malaby reported that 20 percent of the working time was allocated to so-called secret projects. Each employee was expected to develop his creativity by working on a personal idea, even if this idea did not lead to any result in the end.[11] However, in the Korean company, there was apparently no such expectation from either hierarchy or workers regarding creativity.

Those sketchbooks were kept hidden most of the time, but they were also regularly shown to the members of the team, and pages were uploaded in online communities in order to get feedback from peers. The role of peers has often been overlooked in research on learning processes, but is important to consider.[12] The possibilities offered by information technologies has made peer networks more visible, especially in East Asia where professional and amateur productions are closely connected with each other. For my interviewees, the feedback provided by peers was mutual and continuous; it was taken very seriously, certainly more than the feedback provided by the hierarchy at their paid work. These manhwaga seemed to share what Mizuko Itô describes as "amateur ethos": a valuation of a type of work that is free of constraints and is acknowledged by peers.[13] They were not training on their own as disconnected or marginal individuals but involved in a complex weaving of social groups. However, their networks comprised mostly, when not exclusively, professionals—namely people who were paid for drawing. Their position in game companies, while apparently not valued, contributed in their legitimacy as *professional* illustrators. While the company was openly denigrated for the objects that it produced, it was an important space where networks of peers grew and where statuses evolved.

Personal projects are an integral part of the creative industries. Even when not published, they are considered an asset, a virtue, a sign of commitment. This tends to blur the lines between work and leisure. The main goal of personal projects is a never-ending improvement of the worker, as indicated in the use of the word "training" *(yeonseup)*: these illustrators *trained* their body in order to develop an ability to materialize the pictures that they had in mind. I would like to stress that peers were not equal in this self-realization process. In this company, graphic designers mentioned a "hierarchy of creation" that echoes the theory of the pyramid in arts:[14] the artistic director was at the top and the animators were at the bottom. Animators in this company were not in charge of character or background design but only of animating effects and character movements. They were indeed younger, had more women, and were considered temporary and replaceable. The animators were not involved in the decisions; they did not keep personal sketchbooks in the workplace and expressed stronger concern about the possible loss of their drawing skills.

Conclusion

Indeed, many people who draw for a living—the majority of them—generally work under the orders of an art director or artist in charge. Their work should thus not be analyzed only under the regimes of intention or talent but could also be understood as a highly skilled profession. Even if many of these employees aspire to create their own manhwa and spare some time for their training, most of their working time is spent doing something other than drawing their own project. The fact that some of them do not have personal projects, sometimes because of a lack of time, should not disqualify them as manhwaga.

Even if there is a "hierarchy of creation" acknowledged by everyone in the company, all members of the graphics team nonetheless share a common professional culture that is heavily influenced by comics in general, including Japanese manga, American cartoons, and French illustration. The common point of this large culture lies in drawings characters and the worlds surrounding them. As per my interviewees, many Korean illustrators are not particularly willing to praise national manhwa as opposed to Japanese manga, and they have no problem with using Japanese references at an individual level. While some artists are involved in the defense of their national manhwa culture, their political choice is merely one among many others. I would assert that "drawing" consists first and foremost of a technique of the body, which invites us to consider the community of manhwaga not only as a community of fans but also as what educational theorist Etienne Wenger calls a "community of practice."[15] Contrary to communities formed around shared passions (such as fandoms), local entities (such as villages or diasporas), or common goals (for example, the renovation of a monument or the organization of a performance), where tasks and skills are distributed among individuals, communities of practice are united by a common skilled activity and clearly oriented toward learning. Here, the community of manhwaga is essentially defined by an education of the body that is perceived as relying more on a horizontal structure among peers than on a classical vertical structure between master and apprentice. Refining this technique of the body, in order to reach mastery and then use this mastery to express one's own ideas and style, is at the core of the manhwaga's work, both for the needs of their personal projects and for the needs of the various projects (games, anime, etc.) that they work for during their careers.

The value of technical mastery could be understood as a sign of a contemporary work culture[16] that praises self-realization and "artification"—that is, the fact that a growing number of professions tend to borrow material, institutional and ideological settings from the arts, and eventually transform into arts.[17] Several Western countries have tried to label games and comics as arts, mainly by displaying their great graphical quality through dedicated exhibitions. In the meantime, many artists and game designers reject this focus on graphics and produce experimental projects, which are hybrids of games and artworks. Artification is complex and intertwined with legitimation issues. However, in South Korea, the legitimization of manhwaga's work seems to follow different paths. It should be noted that, for several decades, numerous artists (such as musicians or film directors) have claimed to be craftsmen or entertainers rather than artists. In this regard, and referring to both art historian Jacqueline Berndt's invitation to consider the manual craft of Japanese manga[18] and to similarities between the activities of artists and craftsmen (such as the musicians and masons depicted by social anthropologist Marc Perrenoud),[19] I propose an analysis of the profession of manhwaga as a type of craftsmanship, which involves specific rules, including stylistic rules. When I first looked at the "personal sketches" that illustrators showed to me, what seemed striking to me was, first, the amazing skills of almost every member of the graphic team and, second, a relative homogeneity. All "personal projects" could look very similar at first. While a handful of personal projects showed very unique styles, the vast majority shared a lot of common graphical codes that were heavily influenced by manga and games.

It should be noted that homogeneity is not limited to this specific team or company: it has been analyzed as a major component of manga culture by researchers who highlighted the strong conventions and the advanced codification of manga and anime.[20] The personal projects could look conformist, but they were considered by the authors as reflecting their own personal style. It is only after a few weeks that I could distinguish them from each other; those with a trained eye could see this personal touch immediately. Each illustrator had a style that consisted of subtle, micro-innovations, variations within a precise set of aesthetic and technical rules. This configuration evokes the work of craftsmen whose work relies mainly on mastering techniques and implicit rules while adding a personal touch that only experts can detect. It also evokes, to some extent, certain categories of artists such as classical musicians who can add their personal touch within a very subtle range of possibilities, while following an elaborate set of rules and mastering specific skills to a high level of virtuosity. They are often considered (and sometimes consider themselves) as interpreters rather than artists, relying on a limited definition of art, which gives priority to creation, originality, and innovation.

Another argument in favor of the craftsmanship approach lies in the never-ending self-improvement. Every manhwaga in this company effectively worked to improve his skills, either by the means of personal projects or by looking for tasks, which would be educational for them. In the interviews, they insisted on their aspiration to create a perfect manga; but in everyday practices, their efforts were mainly directed at improving their technique. Their quest for virtuosity involved negotiations on working hours and allocated tasks. The members of the graphic team, next to their paid work, either at home or during free time in the workplace, were developing two qualities: their craft, and their freedom. While they often complained about the constraints associated with the workplace and dreamed of better working environments, they were mainly busy trying to free themselves from the constraints of their own body. One of them explained that the most frustrating thing for him was being unable to express the images that were in his head. In order to overcome this difficulty, he aspired to get better at drawing. The technical skills, actively constructed, can thus be considered as a way of emancipation from the limitations of the body. The possibilities of refining one's technical skills could be one of the reasons why graphic designers tend to consider the manga industry as a professional path that is superior to the videogame industry and renowned for producing better images and for being more demanding. Even if entering the competitive manhwa industry does not necessarily mean becoming an author, it means working with fellow craftsmen, which comes with collectively producing more valuable products and improving one's skills. This taste for excellence and well-executed work can be found in most crafts where it plays a central role in decisions regarding the choice of workplace, projects, colleagues, tools and materials, for example.

Considering illustrators as craftsmen could also contribute to understanding the Korean artists' relation to Japan. We have seen that Japanese manga was one of the main reasons why these illustrators gained their passion for drawing. It is at the core of their professional culture, where it is considered the norm to speak Japanese, at least to some extent, to enjoy various aspects of Japanese culture and to befriend Japanese people. In South Korea, the general image of Japan is tainted by the atrocities committed throughout history and by the choices made by today's Japanese government, and so positive attitudes toward Japan can raise suspicion. However, in this professional context, no such suspicion is expressed. The reference to Japanese manga artists is self-evident, and the unavoidable reference to Japan is explained by the fact that illustrators in Japan have been producing these types of works for a long time. The manhwaga thus construct the idea of a Japanese tradition (among others) for manga, which they can rely on and participate in.

The reference to a Japanese "tradition" of manga also builds up the idea of craftsmanship, where it is expected that craftsmen travel to emblematic places in order to refine their craft. Craftsmanship places excellence as a goal beyond all national affiliations. In the same manner as craftsmen have been traveling to countries, regions, or cities famous for a specific production—for example, Japanese craftsmen have been traveling to Lyon, France, to learn from its advanced silk industry after the Meiji Restoration,[21] and before that to other places such as Ichon, Korea, for ceramics or Gyeongju for gold and silver work.[22] Many young Europeans temporarily settle in Switzerland to learn from masters of watch-making, or in Mirecourt, France, to study wood-instrument making. Travel is at the core of several traditional craftsmen organizations such as the Compagnons du Devoir in France, where aspiring craftsmen are required to join masters and places renowned for a specific craft. Following the same pattern, South Korean illustrators seek places where they can learn among the most skilled workers. Traditional craftsmen are not usually accused of being copycats or traitors when they travel abroad to learn from skilled masters and incorporate technical and stylistic elements in their further work. Korean manhwaga, on the contrary, have to deal with such accusations since the visible Japaneseness is perceived as endangering the possibility of Koreanness.[23] More important, they have to answer assignations of identities, which are supposedly national (rather than, for example, related to a specific region or city). This frame allows us to understand why many South Korean illustrators are not very enthusiastic when it comes to fitting into or building fixed national "identities." They see themselves as part of a community of craftsmen, which has tinges of transnational elements to it. In the long run, the qualities that they see in Japanese manga are dynamic tools to improve their skills and eventually express their own ideas, and their relation to Japanese society opens a breach for changing society at the smaller level of a craft profession.

....

Chloé Paberz received her PhD in social anthropology from Paris Nanterre University in 2016. Her research focuses on the creative work processes of the emblematic objects of South Korean modernity. Her PhD dissertation, based on the ethnography of a videogame company, describes how creative workers manage the setbacks and frustration that occur during the process of designing a game. She has been conducting research on how artists and innovators deal with the demand of creating "something Korean" in foreign countries—first in France with a RESCOR fellowship at EHESS's Center for Korean studies in Paris, then in Japan under a JSPS program at Ritsumeikan University in Kyôto, and finally in the UK with a fellowship from the Korea Foundation at SOAS, University of London. She is now Associate Professor at the University of Languages and Civilizations (Inalco) in Paris.

....

Acknowledgments

I would like to thank the Japan Society for the Promotion of Science and the Korea Foundation who supported the writing of the first drafts of this paper, and the French Ministry of Superior Education and Research, which provided funding for the early stage or this research (described in my PhD dissertation: Chloé Paberz, "La cité des héros. Ethnographie d'une petite entreprise de jeux vidéo en Corée du Sud," Thèse de doctorat en Ethnologie, Université Paris Nanterre, 2016).

Notes

The names of the interviewees have been changed, except for the informants who explicitly required to appear under their real names. In accordance with *Mechademia* style, all Korean words follow the official Revised Romanization of Korean. "Korean" refers to "South Korean" throughout this paper.

1. Jaqueline Berndt, "Preface," in *Manhwa, Manga, Manhua: East Asian Comics Studies*, ed. Jaqueline Berndt (Leipzig: Leipziger Universitätsvlg, 2012), 7–9.
2. Sophie Houdart, "*La cour des miracles: ethnologie d'un laboratoire japonais*," in *Le travail créateur: S'accomplir dans l'incertain*, ed. Pierre-Michel Menger (Paris: Gallimard, Le Seuil, 2009).
3. Emmanuel Grimaud, Sophie Houdart, and Denis Vidal, "*Artifices et effets spéciaux*," *Terrain. Revue d'ethnologie de l'Europe*, no. 46 (March 2006): 5–14.
4. Kim Soo-jung, *Agigongnyong dulli*, 13 episodes (Seoul: KBS, 1987–88).
5. Yoo Soo-Kyung, "On Differences Between Japanese and Korean Comics for Female Readers: Comparing 'Boys Over Flowers' to 'Goong,'" in *Manhwa, Manga, Manhua: East Asian Comics Studies*, ed. Jacqueline Berndt (Leipzig: Leipziger Universitätsvlg, 2012).
6. Berndt, "Preface."
7. Chloé Paberz, "The Narrative of the Misfit among South Korean Game Developers," in *Korean Screen Cultures: Interrogating Cinema, TV, Music and Online Games*, ed. Andrew David Jackson and Colette Balmain, 55–76 (Bern: Peter Lang, 2016).
8. Michael Lucken, "Le Japon singe," in *Les Fleurs artificielles: Création, imitation et logique de domination*, AsieS (Paris: Presses de l'Inalco, 2016), 17–29.
9. Geneviève Delbos and Paul Jorion, *La transmission des savoirs* (Éditions de la Maison des sciences de l'homme, 1984).
10. Marcel Mauss, "Les techniques du corps," in *Sociologie et Anthropologie* (Paris: Presses Universitaires de France, 1950), 365–86.
11. Thomas M. Malaby, *Making Virtual Worlds: Linden Lab and Second Life* (Ithaca: Cornell University Press, 2009).
12. Alice Doublier, "La texture du monde: Apprendre la céramique dans une université d'art de Kyôto" (Thèse de doctorat en Ethnologie, Université Paris Nanterre, 2017).

13. Mizuko Itô Okabe, Daisuke, Tsuji, Izumi, *Fandom Unbound: Otaku Culture in a Connected Age* (New Haven: Yale University Press, 2012).

14. Pierre-Michel Menger, *Le travail créateur: S'accomplir dans l'incertain* (Paris: Gallimard, Le Seuil, 2009).

15. Etienne Wenger, *Communities of Practice: Learning, Meaning, and Identity* (Cambridge: Cambridge University Press, 1999.

16. Dominique Méda, "Comment mesurer la valeur accordée au travail?" *Sociologie* 1, no. 1 (April 2010): 121-40.

17. Nathalie Heinich and Roberta Shapiro, *De l'artification: Enquêtes sur le passage à l'art* (Paris: Editions de l'Ecole des Hautes Etudes en Sciences Sociales, 2012).

18. Jaqueline Berndt, "Hand in Hand: *Kouno Fumiyos Mangaserie Kono sekai no katasumi ni* (In This Corner of the World) *im Vergleich zur Anime-Adaptation durch Katabuchi Sunao*" (Berlin: De Gruyter Open, 2018), 53-84.

19. Marc Perrenoud, "Les musicos au miroir des artisans du bâtiment," *Ethnologie française* 38, no. 1 (February 2008): 101-6.

20. Stevie Suan, "Anime's Performativity: Diversity through Conventionality in a Global Media-Form," *Animation* 12, no. 1 (March 2017): 62-79.

21. Tomoko Hashino and Keijiro Otsuka, *Industrial Districts in History and the Developing World* (New York: Springer, 2016).

22. Edward B. Adams, *Korean Folk Art and Craft* (Tuttle Pub, 1987); Andre Eckardt, *A History of Korean Art* (London: Edward Goldston, 1929).

23. Yoo Soo-Kyung, "On Differences Between Japanese and Korean Comics for Female Readers"; Chie Yamanaka, "Domesticating Manga? National Identity in Korean Comics Culture," in *Reading Manga: Local and Global Perceptions of Japanese Comics*, ed. Jaqueline Berndt and Steffi Richter (Leipzig: Leipzig University Press, 2006).

Anime's Spatiality

Media-form, Dislocation, and Globalization

STEVIE SUAN

Medium, Material, Convention

In an analysis of how anime has been explored in academia, Jaqueline Berndt delineates two important strands in anime research: area studies (namely, Japan studies) and media studies. Regarding the former, Berndt describes a tendency to focus on the social context of anime, to explore societal issues in Japan as they are represented in anime.[1] This methodology, like all methodologies, has certain tendencies. Specifically, Berndt notes how the givenness of anime to represent Japanese society is often taken for granted, where anime is mined for sociological readings of Japan without consideration of its mode of expression.[2] In such cases, anime acts as the "medium" in the sense of a conduit through which one views Japan, an invisible "in-between" or middle, the channel through which something about Japan is conveyed.

Media studies, however, investigates a different notion of "medium": anime as animation. For example, Deborah Levitt examines anime-esque works to explore the dynamics of the medium more broadly. With almost no reference to Japan, Levitt explores animation in terms of its an-ontology, that is, how "animation must always create a world" from nothing, and in this sense "is not tethered to a grounding model . . . everything is shadowed by its possible metamorphosis, erasure, and resurrection—and there is thus no ontology."[3] Though this is Levitt's central concern, she notes something similar to Berndt's observations on anime as invisible in-between, stating that "conventions within animation itself have developed in different genres and national traditions of animation, and where these are used without comment, they also become 'invisible.'" Yet Levitt asserts that animation still has the ability to "comment on conventional codes of figuration and representation, as well as to reflect upon the existential, perceptual coordinates they conventionally represent."[4]

However, there is still more to the story of anime's medium, as it is also important to consider how the specifics of materials can matter to the medium in question. While Levitt notes the significance of materiality, in the current context, Thomas Lamarre's work in *The Anime Machine,* can be read as an exploration of how attending to the materiality of anime's animation, the manipulation of its celluloid layers, and can reveal philosophical insights into the medium. According to Lamarre, in TV anime's approach, in its brand of limited animation, the multiple layers are spread flat across the sequence of images, the force of the movement shunted to the surface.[5] One product of this type of animating appears in character design, what Lamarre labels the "soulful body," where the potentiality for movement as well as "spiritual, emotional, or psychological qualities appear inscribed on the surface."[6] Such characters are "at once unframed and enframed, . . . as if all the depth brought to the surface became condensed into one soulful figure, allowing it to flash from media to media."[7]

As such, soulful bodies are not limited to celluloid animation but are "stretched across innumerable platforms and fields" in the media mix.[8] This media mix, as Marc Steinberg has detailed, is central to many of the developments of anime's aesthetics, and characters and their designs are integral to this dynamic. To ease the integration of various mediums (comics, stickers, figurines, etc.), a certain type of posing of the character has also proliferated, what Steinberg labels as "dynamic immobility," the sense of potential for movement caught in the pose of the character's body.[9] Combining Lamarre and Steinberg's concepts, the soulful bodies of these characters and their poses in dynamic immobility enable them to move with relative ease between mediums and materials in the media mix.

But this dynamic between medium and material gets further complicated with anime. Due to the prominence of the above-mentioned designs and poses, certain kinds of characters and poses have become conventionalized through their continued repetition across different media, producing character design models and poses, which is now associated with anime. Read through the framework explored here, the material interacts with the repetition of convention: the technical engagement with the material via limited animation affords a certain type of character design and posing that, in turn, becomes repeated as the soulful body and poses of dynamic immobility; such designs and poses also respond to the various other mediums and materials they are repeatedly performed with in the media mix. This dynamic is also not linear; which one causes the next interaction is not necessarily clear. For example, anime's conventions are also performed in computer graphics (CG) to produce recognizable "anime" shows and films, adjusting and creating new technologies to do so—in this case, the prior conventions are inducing shifts in the different materials and methods of animation to sustain a certain media product.

This element of recognizability and conventionality is important to consider as TV anime are increasingly produced in larger and larger numbers, identifiable as a distinctive category of media inside and outside of Japan. In order to maintain itself as such a category, anime must continue to reiterate these design patterns within a particular register (e.g., the soulful body in the poses of dynamic immobility, the types of line work, body shapes, and facial expressions, among other elements), constraining anime within those parameters, even as it changes over time. Should the designs stray too far from the recognizable patterns, they risk becoming unidentifiable as "anime." There is, then, a tension in the iterations of anime characters, where they must reference prior designs to be recognizable but not be redundant or unrecognizable (and therefore potentially unsellable). In this sense, every anime is in a taut and tense relationship with prior anime, citing earlier instances that are external to that particular anime (that is, "citing" from what Azuma Hiroki calls a "database"),[10] while keeping some sense of specificity in its current instantiation. Here, I use the examples of character design and poses, but many of the elements considered recognizably anime-esque (e.g., narrative patterns, animation techniques) enact this dynamic as well. In other words, this is how anime performatively constitutes its identity, through repeating these anime-esque elements.[11]

In sum, anime's relationship with medium, material, and convention is complex, as they are all interrelated (though not necessarily in this order): there are certain tendencies that occur through the engagement with the material and technology (historically celluloid and the multiplanar animation stand), conventionalized through reiterations, whose citation in other examples (other anime, media mix products, fan works, etc.) invite us to produce groupings of repetitions of these examples (anime series or films) that substantiate some idea of a cohesiveness to anime, which in this article is mainly limited to the performance in the medium of animation (cel and CG). This (nonlinear) interplay between medium, material, and convention, which produces the recognizability of anime, may be termed anime's "media-form" and considered as something performatively constituted through the above-mentioned repetition.[12]

It is with this point of departure that I return to the question of anime's relation to Japan, examining the mechanics of the performance of anime's media-form that, contrary to a concrete grounding as Japanese, is instead replete with an anxiety about situatedness, an unease between locality and globality, internal and external. These tensions, characteristic of the contemporary moment of globalization, will be revealed through an examination of the performance of anime's media-form: in the dynamics of the medium of animation, the material realities of anime's production, and the repetition of conventions to ensure recognizability. In this interplay between medium, material, and convention, anime performance enacts a particular type of spatiality whereby it becomes increasingly difficult to securely locate and ground oneself as an individual subject in the classical sense inherited from modernity.

What I mean here by spatiality is not represented "space" but a way of organizing and situating ourselves within space (and time).[13] In this sense, modernity is itself a historical regime of spatiality, deeply connected with the rise of the modern nation-state, of organizing, producing, and imposing borders on geographic space, which in turn produce identities grounded in the culture of that nation. But anime's performance of media-form does not insist on the neat, ordered world of the nation-state or modern selfhood; on multiple different levels anime employs the complex spatiality of contemporary globalization. Enacted through anime's performance of its media-form, this spatiality may be examined as another (but concurrent) mode of existence that engenders different forms of selfhood, relations to the nation-state, and approaches to geography altogether, a reorganization of how to conceive of the world.

For anime, this is governed by a tension between Japan (anime as Japanese cultural product, as representing Japan) and the global (of anime across the world), occurring on multiple registers: in the very performance of the media-form itself (which straddles the tensions of multiplicity and uniformity in each iterable performance), in the enactment of characters (constituted by the execution of conventionalized expressions that themselves deal with the tensions of iterability), of existing at multiple places at once (on and outside the characters), in the type of movements enabled (by working with/through the multiple layers that are composited to make up the singular anime image), and through the transnational production processes (where these layers are produced in multiple places at different times). Thus, anime enacts a spatiality that is constituted through a connection to other locales in its very performance of media-form, encapsulating the frictions of globalization and the problematic of situating oneself. This spatiality of dislocation—that is, situated in a particular location but somehow also displaced due to its relation to iterations elsewhere—engages with the tensions of dispersal and unity; a singular point becoming the site of an accumulation of diverse relations, a node in a network, always connecting to other instances in other spaces. By examining this spatiality, it is possible to see how even place-focused anime enact the problematics of dislocation, apparently situated in a particular location yet also displaced elsewhere.

Dislocation in Enacting Anime Characters

In order to better explicate this spatiality, let me provide some examples that display this dynamic, taking specific instances from the anime series *Macross Frontier* (TV series, 2008; films, 2009, 2011). First, it is worth considering the manner in which anime enacts selfhood, where the characters utilize a repertoire of preestablished conventionalized codes to display their emotion. For instance, there is a particular scene at the end of episode 5, where the entire sequence is made up of each character (Alto, Sheryl, and Ranka) performing conventional codes in their interactions with one another (Figure 1). Each of their facial expressions and gestures performed in that sequence are not unique to those individual characters but rather codified, preestablished before the characters enacted them. Many such codes optimize the stillness and jerkiness of limited animation, rapidly switching between these codes, which often employ poses that are "dynamic-immobile" in their expressive capacity despite their relative stillness. Several of these codes are well-known clichés of anime's conventions, including the arched eyes for happiness and the glimmering eyes. These two expressions are so common that they are sometimes used as stereotypes for the way anime characters express themselves. Indeed, two characters (Sheryl and Ranka) both perform the same expression (glimmering eyes) in this scene.

This "citing" also occurs across genres and production companies. For example, the gesture of placing a hand on the cheek that has been kissed can be seen in episode 20 of *Death Note* (2006-7), when Misa kisses the character L. The situation and facial expressions are not exactly the same as in the *Macross Frontier* scene where Sheryl kisses Alto, but the gesture itself is the one regularly performed for situations when a character unexpectedly kisses another on the cheek. The softening of the facial expression is also commonly performed to express a sudden endearment to another character, making the

Figure 1. Screen captures of each expression in this scene, which is a performance of a conventional code by Alto, Sheryl, and Ranka in episode 5 of *Macross Frontier*.

performance of Alto's reaction to Sheryl's kiss a combination of two different expressions. This method of performance, where characters combine citations of preexisting codes has been labeled "figurative acting" by Donald Crafton.[14] Anime characters tend to maintain a somewhat strict repetition of these figurative acting codes, never straying too far from imitating earlier instances of those codes, as in the *Macross Frontier* example above. This is because, like many of the conventions in anime, should the performance of these codes diverge too far from the prior iterations, they would become illegible.

What is important for the purposes here is that the figurative acting performed in anime produces a type of character that is entirely made up of citations of preexisting codes that exist outside of that particular character. This is distinct from what Crafton calls "embodied acting" which is found in animation like Disney's or Pixar's works, where the characters have unique and individualized movements that appear to come naturally from inside of the character to express their emotions outwardly. Because the codes that are cited by anime characters are external to the characters performing them, there is an inside-outside dynamic in which the distinctions among internal and external become thoroughly blurred. Anime characters' expressions are cited from outside of their somatic boundaries, and when enacted appear "on" (not "in") them, similar to the interiority inscribed on their surfaces in the designs of their soulful bodies. The performance of character becomes something of an accumulation of different types of codes and the frequency through which they are cited from the repertoire (or database) of anime's figurative acting codes. Localized in their iterations of that specific character, this combination of cited codes is what produces their personality and selfhood. It is difficult to concretely isolate an enactment of the code to that singular instance, as its very operations of legibility are sustained by its recognizable relation to earlier instances by other characters in different anime. Subsequently, there is a tension between the localized, situated moment of these cited codes and their other, external instances of their enactment.

This produces a type of spatiality where there is a definitive relation to prior, external iterations of the codes, as well as the particularized enactment of that code for that character in that specific space at that moment. In other words, a combination of different times and locales of earlier and even contemporaneous enactments of those codes are not only externally present but also localized in that particular location. This is a starkly different type of spatial organization for selfhood than the individualism inherited from modernity, which maintains a discrete inside/outside and is grounded as human in their singular body in that localized space. Instead, anime's enactment of characters (through performing anime's media-form) operates through the type of spatiality described above, engaging with the problematic of dislocation: the character is indistinct, localized in that particular spatiotemporal location but at the same time connected to a network of instantiations of the elements that produce that character.[15]

In general, an anime performance as a whole operates according to similar dynamics, each anime citing prior examples to maintain recognizability, reiterating them in differing combinations. As such, anime might be described as theatrical in the sense that Samuel Weber defines it through his exploration of the medium of theater. For Weber, the idea of theater as medium finds a particularly important articulation in staging and acting, where he observes a great unease about space, time, and reality.[16] According to Weber, stages are not only in their current locale but also a "stage" in the temporal sense of moving toward something else, a localization that is always haunted by earlier instances, other stages, or as shifting between multiple locales in one place. To be staged (i.e., to be performed on stage, to enact in the locale par excellence of the medium of theater) implies a connection to other instances.[17] Acting also takes on a similar disjointedness in regard to space and time. For Weber, "acting" is very different from "action," which implies a completeness to it, a concreteness that "acting" seems to imitate. Instead, acting "is intrinsically open and indeterminable, determinable only with respect to the space-time of its enunciation."[18] In short, staging and acting, crucial components of what can be considered the medium of theater, are divisible in some sense, divided between the here and now and some other space and time—thus the unease felt by many regarding theater's relationship to reality. Theatricality, then, is not necessarily in the physical material of a stage or actor but invokes the problematic of the self-identical and the multiple in the singular: theatricality as medium insists on a tension involving repetition that plays itself out in each performance.

This theatrical engagement with repetition and reality further relates to anime in regard to the an-ontological dimension that Levitt describes: of animation as a medium and its reliance on convention. For Levitt, animation explores a type of simulacrum, which does not directly replicate reality but is an encounter with images that "have left the realm in which a reality principle holds sway."[19] Unlike cinema, which is grounded in the human body, in animation an entirely different dynamic unfolds, where the operations of situating oneself on concrete ground become difficult. In consideration of this, in the performance of anime's media-form, which relies so heavily on conventionality in both character acting and sustaining anime's recognizability generally, one can find a similar unease toward a grounding of space (and time).

For anime, this corresponds with the tensions of theatricality, between multiplicity and unity, between repetition and variation in the citations of conventions. Through this constitutive process, anime performance fuses together different times and different locations of previously enacted iterations as a combination of citations in their current placement. Even when actualized in a specific anime character's figurative performance, this form of selfhood is distinct from the modern individual—whose localized inside/outside boundaries forge identities that easily align with the spatiality of the "container model" of the nation-state—and consequently has a very different relation to locale. Inside and outside become blurred, where the execution of each iteration somehow links beyond that localized space of its performance (extending beyond singular characters, episodes, even studios and various media). In consideration of this, anime's spatiality may provide insights into how to consider a different conception of place and our relation to it under globalization—a topic I return to later.

Difficulty Situating Oneself

To further our investigation of the problematic of situating oneself, I would like to turn to Lamarre's discussion on the visuality of anime's animations, in particular the missile barrages (with trailing streams of smoke) that swerve toward and away from their rapidly moving target. Sometimes called the "Itano Circus" after animator Itano Ichirô who first performed them in cel animation, these missile barrages are a hallmark of mecha anime, they are particularly associated with the *Macross* franchise, appearing in every series, including *Macross Frontier*, even though it is executed in CG. Describing the dynamics of an early instance of the missile barrages in the *Daicon IV Opening Animation* (1983), Lamarre relates it to a type of compositing of the multiplanar image afforded by cel animation's utilization of layers. In this case, there is an engagement with what he calls the "exploded view/projection"—when the force of the moving image is spread across the flat plane of the image, creating a particular structure of depth that differs from Cartesian one-point perspective: "the controlled quasi-orthogonal structural 'explosion' of elements across the image surface."[20] The swerving movements of the missiles, as they converge and diverge on the moving target, produce an emergent depth through their manipulation of the various layers across the image's surface. The missiles veer in and out of Cartesian one-point perspective, suggesting but also perverting it. The sequence thus produces emergent depth by engaging with technical solutions to the issues of compositing the multiplanar image, and is a revealing example of a larger tendency where movement into depth is replaced by density of information, where "structures of exploded projection emerge to place a material limit on dispersion and flatness, generating temporary fields of potential depth associated with lines of sight."[21]

In sequences like this, the movement of the projectiles flattens the hierarchy of the image associated with modernity. Lamarre notes how, distinct from Cartesian one-point perspective, this "shows how something can be taken apart or put together." The potential depths operate as fields, functioning similar to the dynamics of information retrieval, where viewers skim and scan, and the potential depths "if pursued, promise to generate links and connections."[22] Interestingly, as if displaying this exact dynamic, in episode 7 of *Macross Frontier*, before the missiles are shot, a close-up shows the pilot's eyes scanning for targets that the missiles then track. Similarly, the viewer becomes an "interactor who intermittently situates herself within the assemblage, adopting the angle of different components. This is not so much viewing positions as lines of sight . . . that constitute different trajectories across the assemblage," implying "a capture of the multiplicity within unity . . . an inherent oscillation between . . . dispersion and capture."[23] As such, the viewer scanning this moving image does not sustain "a one-point structuration to produce depth with distinct positioning."[24]

Lamarre notes that the Daicon animations might be considered as "poised at a moment of technological transition, from the nation-centered military industrial complex to transnational flows of information," providing a point of departure for exploring how this relates to globalization.[25] To do so, and to return to the theatrical dynamics of enacting characters in anime, one might connect this to some of the observations by Paul Virilio, who describes a shift in the problematic of actors due to the global reach of certain technologies. Traditionally, the rapid shifts between characters and the lives that actors portray invited the question of "Who am I?" In this problematic, there is a layering (a doubling) on the body of the actor, where the actor as person is inhabited by the character (which appears to come from outside), and confusion between these two incites the question of identity (which is classically singular). But due to the contemporary difficulty of orienting oneself in space, Virilio suggests that this question has now transformed into the problem of "Where am I?" and is transposed onto users of different technologies.

This is in part because various technologies (both communicative and transportation oriented) now circumnavigate and interconnect the globe at speeds that seem to render all points of location (even on the earth's surface itself) difficult to sustain as concretely grounded. In other words, in this historical moment, suffused with technologies and globalized on multiple levels, there is a distinctive problematic of how and where to situate ourselves. Classical concepts of time and space have become confused through our contemporary modes of perception through technology, where a livestream can muddy past recording, present viewing, and future responses into a singular "now." Moreover, such live-streams can be interacted with in real-time from any place on (or above) the planet without any physical displacement from our current location: "motion *on the spot* instead of motion *in space*."[26] In this manner, the actor (or users of communications technologies among other technologies), is overlain with a multitude of temporal and spatial coordinates, producing a dislocation of the actor. Thus, it is not so much the literal question of "Where am I" that is actually considered by users but rather the problematic the question opens up—one of how and where to situate oneself—that is important to consider at the current time. With this in mind, the performance of anime's media-form can be seen as engaging with a politics of examining these problematics: of the difficulty (if not impossibility via classical means) of situating oneself in our current era, especially in consideration of the transnational flows of globalization.

Anime's Media Heterotopia

Yet, anime is generally conceived of as grounded or situated in relation to Japan. The above detailed conventional elements might not be explicitly acknowledged as containers of Japanese culture, but their repetition becomes recognizable as elements of a media-form that has become promoted and predominantly received as a Japanese cultural product globally. However, closer inspection of the materiality and conventionality of performing anime's media-form can reveal a transnational complexity, specifically in its production processes. Indeed, the material conditions of anime's animation, having developed from the multiplanar images afforded by the layers of celluloid animation, lends itself very well to the transnational distribution of labor: different layers can be produced by different people (e.g., key-animation and backgrounds can be done in different places at different times), and then composited into a single image, which contributes to the massive reliance on freelancers and subcontractors in the industry, creating a network of production that extends beyond single studios located in one nation.

As the various layers of an anime image can be produced across multiple nations, one anime's animation-sequence may have been story-boarded in Japan, the background painted in Vietnam, key-animation done in South Korea and Japan, character in-betweens in China, then colored in the Philippines, and edited in Japan, merging the multiple locales of each part's production into the single images that make up the sequence. For example, episode 6 of *Macross Frontier* had storyboarding, key animation, CG, and compositing done at various studios in Japan (often at studio Satelight), but the labor also included additional key-animation work by studio Daejin (South Korea), French set director Stanislas Brunet in Japan, animation and finishing work by KMU Manila Studio (Philippines), ShangJie Animation and Zizidongman (PRC), and backgrounds by Biho (Japan and Vietnam). Therefore, while specifics of which exact images come from where are not often explicated, some parts of that particular episode have elements produced in different national locales but composited together.

From this perspective, it is possible to see how anime's animation that is outsourced throughout Asia is not only part of a transnational performance but also one that tends to flow through Japan. In particular, Tokyo (and to a lesser extent Osaka and Kyoto) operates as what Michael Curtin calls a "media capital," a transnational center that has secured a prominence in the regional or global production and circulation of media.[27] It is along these lines that Tokyo functions as the central node in a larger Asian production network, making anime's transnationally produced images what Hye Jean Chung calls a "media heterotopia":

> A mediated space of representation created by compositing multiple layers that contain spectral residues of dispersed geographical locations and laboring bodies. As a result, bits and pieces of the material world— that is, traces of sites and bodies of production—are embedded, or woven, into the film's texture, thus belying the aesthetic and rhetorical emphasis on seamlessness that glosses over any conflicts or frictions.[28]

The compositing process of the multiple layers of the image tends to rely on erasure of the labor-intensive production process, and cognizance of this multilayered component of the image allows us to rediscover this history and tension in the supposedly seamless image.[29] The audiovisual composite of anime performance, the media heterotopia of anime, then, does not really come from any single place but rather embodies a tension between multiple places of production in its unified images.

But Chung focuses on live-action cinema, where actual indexical elements of locations can be identified. Anime, as animation, is different, as each layer of the image has to be created from the ground up. Because of anime's fabricated nature as animation, it is far easier to disguise the location of the labor of production, so long as the conventions of anime have been reproduced. A unity can be achieved through the organized execution of similar (visual) conventions: the uniformity enacted through the performance of anime as a media-form. Seeing anime as a performative media heterotopia is an attempt to bring the layers of production into view, providing a degree of agency to the performers while acknowledging the impositions (and constraints) through which they perform. Viewed in this way, anime's heterotopic images constantly balance a tension between the multiplicity of geographically disparate places, people, and materials involved in the production and their unity in the conventions used to produce the images of anime.

While I am highlighting a perception of unity, I would like to make it clear that this unity is not one without its own frictions and hierarchies, with the relation to Japan bearing incredible weight in this dynamic. The media-form of anime that the workers are performing, under current conceptions of anime, is overtly acknowledged and promoted as Japanese culture, forcing foreign animators to produce animation that is visibly recognizable as from another culture. Even if the animators are credited (which was not always the case), there are further problems as these subcontractors are often in or from places that have a history of oppression from Japan. While the conventions of anime are externally imposed on all performers, as something they must master, a different relationship to this imposition occurs for many animators outside of Japan. This, as Kukhee Choo has shown, can produce many difficult conflicts, particularly when non-Japanese animators produce domestic animations in the same or similar media-form that they normally do: when they make anime works.[30]

Importantly, it is the very iterability of anime's conventions that allows it to travel, to be repeatable and cross the national and cultural boundaries that it does. This reliance on iterability, on the capacity to be re-performed in a felicitous manner, both enables and masks the transnationality of anime: it can be learned, mastered, repeated, which allows anime to be produced outside of Japan (and by non-Japanese) or in transnational co-productions. But because its recognizability is so deeply associated with Japan, felicity in the performance becomes associated with Japan and veils the transnationality. There is therefore an invisibility of the different locales involved that is afforded by the performance of anime's conventions. In other words, if anime is to be seen here in terms of production locales then anime's performance is spread across Asia, but the material traces of transnational production are masked through the mastery of performing these conventions, which erases the transnationality of anime when anime's media-form is taken exclusively as a symbol of Japanese culture.

With this in mind, one might interpret certain elements of anime's transnationality, such as the opening of a Chinese-owned anime production company in Tokyo, Emon, as an attempt to work around this dynamic, authenticating itself by its location in Japan. This might also evince the effectiveness of Cool Japan's nation-branding discourses (which try to anchor anime in Japan even as it aims to disperse anime globally), as the transnational potentials become captured within national boundaries. In this way, there is a geopolitical clash in the claim to media-form. Indeed, anime's media heterotopia is not without hierarchies, and there are multiple tensions that can arise from this formation. Among them is the question of whether it is possible to conceive of a new geography to engage with this transnational dynamic, which in turn relates to the spatiality of dislocation. This issue is not isolated to anime but extends to the increasingly globalized dynamics of media industries all over the world, although each media (even in the media mix) will have their own formations of transnationality. Accordingly, contrary to the tendency to take for granted the givenness of anime as Japanese cultural product, there is a complex politics of spatiality and place that intersects with the framework of the nation, and is in conflict with the transnational flows that define this moment of globalization, all enacted through the performance of the media-form of anime.

Anime Out-of-place

Up until now I have been engaged with a conception of location in terms of spatiality rather than space in the traditional sense, but it might be productive to explore the idea of "place" in regards to anime, especially as anime tends to be seen as representing Japan as a certain place. Here one might consider Doreen Massey's conception of a "global sense of place." For Massey, place is not simply a static location, but becomes transformed by layers of history that stem from multiple different locales, an intersection of a variety of materials and peoples, coming from disparate and nearby areas, whose specific combination and interaction makes (and re-makes) the place in question.[31] The performance of anime's media-form, as discussed above, enacts a similar dynamic, not just in its media heterotopia of transnational production but also in its character acting and conventionality, as each enactment is a citation of earlier iterations in that specific instance.

Place-based anime, which depicts particular locales within Japan, have become increasingly popular in recent years. A whole industry has grown around the tourism to various areas that have become the basis for backgrounds for certain anime productions. Such inclusions of real-world places increase drastically toward the end of the first decade of the 2000s, specifically with the marketing success of locales in Saitama after the hit anime *Lucky Star* in 2007. This comes at precisely the time that the initiatives of Cool Japan became more apparent and widespread (both inside and outside of Japan). This movement toward highlighting quotidian Japan can be interpreted as a reaction to the now obvious globalization of anime, as an effort to quell the ambivalence in anime's media-form by grounding the images with a supposedly indexical relation to places in Japan.

However, this might be interpreted as attempting to mask the insecurities of place, of hiding *how* the images of a place are produced by highlighting *what* is represented. With Levitt's conception of the simulacrum of animation in mind, one may view the images of quotidian Japan like desperate answers to ground anime in a reality in which it fundamentally cannot be grounded in. This is exacerbated by the global spread of anime, where the anxieties of globalization are reflected in this push toward indexicality of some kind. For Levitt, even when animation does attempt to represent reality, it is always "a meta-discourse on the conventions of realist representation."[32] From this perspective, while the focus on place might be interpreted as an acceptance of anime as a Japanese national media-form, forcing a reading of indexical relation to sites in Japan, another interpretation arises when the production of place itself is considered.

While the quotidian scenes of the local in anime are very susceptible to becoming folded into the image of the national, their specificity—not just an overpass shown in the anime, but the particular angle the background image was based on, focusing on that particular viewing location—can also be taken as an insistence on the particularity of that locale, forcing us to question the exact boundaries of this place and bringing to focus the process of constituting place in general. Indeed, the images of these places are not exactly indexical, as they are often painted or digitally altered to appear uniform in relation to the characters: the background artists perform a production of the location in the anime media-form. The images are stylized in the anime conventional media-form, a performance of anime as the setting for a number of other anime citations. Furthermore, they do not show the entirety of the place itself but sections of it, selected, composed, reconstituted in anime's media-form. In this sense, in the enactment of media-form, these images of place can be seen in the manner of Massey's sense of place, of place as composite. In addition, these settings are set in juxtaposition with other settings, some entirely fictional, others from distant (or relatively close by) places that are then edited together to create the illusion of a unified world-setting for the characters. Fans even post comparisons between the original place and the anime setting online, comparing the two, allowing one to notice both the similarities and the differences. Here again the tensions of place play out in anime, an ambivalence toward securing a location through the performance of anime's media-form, and the same problematic arises: of distinction and uniformity, variation and repetition, dispersal and unity.

Another question arises in light of anime's transnational labor: how can the transnational labor participating in the production of place-based anime be accounted for? Furthermore, what happens when place-based anime are performed outside of Japan, or are about places outside of Japan? When animation self-identical to anime, that is supposed to be Japanese, becomes repeated elsewhere in Asia (or Europe, the United States, etc.), can these works be considered to represent place in the same way anime that feature Japanese places are? In regards to anime made outside of Japan can be indistinguishable, visually at least, from that made within Japan, issues of a type of "mimicry" or cultural appropriation, cultural imperialism, and/or concerns about creativity (in the modern sense of "original" or "culturally unique") and "authenticity" come to the foreground. Thus, the performance of media-form for anime—or anime as it is currently identified, as Japanese culture—becomes imbued with geopolitical implications (especially in Asia), calling into question the prevailing conceptions of cultural production itself, which is so often place and nation-based.

We see many of these issues brought to our attention in the omnibus film *Shikioriori* (*Flavors of Youth*, 2018), an openly transnational anime production that features three short films that take place in different places in China: Shanghai, Guangzhou, and Hunan. Promoted as a production by Japanese studio CoMix Wave (famous for their anime work with Shinkai Makoto, who directed *Your Name* in 2016, popular in both Japan and China) and Haoliners (who own the Emon studio in Tokyo), it is interesting to note that this anime film's production is almost an inverse of the usual structure of transnational production: in this case, the non-Japanese directors and writers are at the top of the hierarchy of production, and much of the animation production was done in Japan (with some work done in Korea). However, in each section of the film, *Shikioriori* is insistent on its recognition as taking place in China, depicting the shifting landscape of China's modernization but following the convention of anime's focus on the minor, quotidian moments and locales.

In both the Hunan and Shanghai short films, we are provided with scenes that display a nostalgia for earlier places: the Hunan section laments the closing (and then reopening) of a particular restaurant, and the bittersweet nature of the passage of time, with backgrounds that show the earlier and now modernized places from the narrator's hometown. In the Shanghai film, we see the transitions (and demolition) of the old, stone-walled sections of the city, and an ironic miscommunication that causes two adolescents to part ways, only to be reunited after the newly renovated sections open. These bittersweet stories, and the lush visual style in which they are presented are trademarks of CoMix Wave's brand. While this is one particular studio's well-known style of enacting the conventions of anime, it is still very recognizably an anime work, despite the explicit setting of China, and we see anime's obvious conventions in each of the films. For instance, the Shanghai section features many tropes of anime's narratives (intense focus on entrance exams, a miscommunication that sends a romance awry) and its final shot of the characters (before an overview of the reformed stone-walls and an image of the Shanghai skyline) is the performance of anime's conventional smile, of arched eyes and tilted head.

In some ways, one can interpret this performance of anime's media-form as attempting to utilize it as capable of expressing the particularities of any place, becoming the invisible conduit through which we can read the distinctive content. In overly optimistic terms, one can see anime as a type of "universal" media-form (or at the minimum, one shared in East Asia) to the extent that we simply focus on the place that is represented. This is similar to the practices of seeing place-based anime as directly portraying Japan, except that this "universalization" of anime estranges it from its exclusive relation to Japan. Here, anime becomes the medium between China and the world (especially as *Shikioriori* is distributed globally by Netflix). In this view, these works are very clearly about the particulars of place in China (specifically food, lifestyle, and architecture), just though anime's media-form.

Yet, it is hard to regard anime's media-form as entirely invisible because, at the minimum, we have to at least acknowledge it, recognize it in some manner as anime to declare either its "universalization" away from or in close relation to Japan. The transnational then comes into view, the film's depictions of place providing an image of what C. J. W. Wee calls an "urban-modern Asia" that "function[s] as a major expression of a shared commonality-in-difference." These images of urban-modern Asia "offer points of transnational connection within the region and a means of generating the sale and circulation of cultural products that can negotiate the zones of national-cultural differences."[33] In this case, there is a particular balance that needs to be attained, where the details of place are specific to these Chinese locales but effectively expressed in anime's media-form. In other words, Chinese cities are presented as containing the same type of quotidian imagery and affective moments as those commonly displayed in anime about (urban) Japan. But

Figure 2. Screen captures of the final images from "Shanghai Koi" from *Shikioriori,* displaying the conventional code for smiling between images of Shanghai.

what allows us to see a "commonality-in-difference" and points us in the direction of Japan and the transnational is not the represented content (which is very clearly about Chinese cities) but the media-form. In fact, these three components (represented content, media-form, and transnationality) are inextricably linked.

Thus, even as *Shikioriori* tries to create a sense of nostalgia for the particulars of those places (Shanghai, Hunan, Guangzhou), the very media-form of its exposition betrays the tensions of dislocation, of how easy it might be to "see Japan" overlaid on the Chinese landscape. This all becomes visible due to the seemingly out-of-place media-form of "Japanese anime" depicting "Chinese modernization." Consequently, it is not just modernization that becomes visible, but its intersection with globalization, and the accompanying spatiality of dislocation. Judgments of the performance in terms of both quality and authenticity shoot off in both directions, back and forth from China and Japan: how felicitous is the performance of media-form, how accurate is the depiction of the Chinese cities? Indeed, the highly polished, nonpolluted imagery of the cities can be interpreted as a continuation of CoMix Wave's characteristic style of anime or an overt attempt at presenting a clean urban image of China, erasing any sense of pollution.

An ambivalence arises here, partly from the inability to concretely place these works, forcing us to question whether what is represented in this image is because of the actual place or if it was expressed in this manner because of anime's commitment to reiterating conventions (which are ostensibly from Japan). As such, Shanghai, Guangzhou, and Hunan each become dislocated in the process. Furthermore, based on the actualities of its production, *Shikio-riori* is a highly transnational work that invites consideration beyond an international framework, where one nation is situated inside another. Here, the very notion of what it means to be transnational needs to be reconsidered. A more media heterotopic approach is required, which necessarily reorganizes our conception of place toward this composited, border-crossing dynamic. From this viewpoint, *Shikioriori* provides us with a complex problematic, revealing a spatiality of dislocation that is emblematic of globalization on multiple levels, dovetailing with the current dynamics of transnationality. This particular film simply draws our attention to this dynamic in a more pronounced manner than other anime, which are also transnational. It just tends to be overlooked.

In consideration of this, let me conclude by clarifying that I am not trying to disparage analyses of anime in terms of Japanese culture and its subsequent sociocultural context or content, approaches that continue to push research on anime in important directions. Rather, my point is to show that, from the standpoint of media-form, there is an alternative view that directs us toward the radically transnational through its spatiality: in the figurative character acting that extends beyond its locale of enactment; in the complex visuality of the animation; in the transnational production network; in the constitution of place. From this perspective, anime is not necessarily isolated to Japan, its globalization not just Japanese culture spread to other countries. With that said, even as I assert the transnational and global dimensions of anime and its enactment of a spatiality of dislocation, I must insist on the prominence of Japan to the dynamic described here—in the history of anime, its cultural relations (inside and outside of Japan), its development on multiple levels (marketing, media mix, language, conventions, etc.), and as central node in the transnational production processes. The difficulty is figuring out how to account for the specifics of anime's transnationality as we acknowledge the importance and weight of Japan in this system.

In fact, the very problem of how to situate anime studies itself is symptomatic of these tensions between local and global, as our institutionalized disciplines of knowledge production, in particular area studies, finds itself built on a spatiality of modern foundations, organized around national frameworks (Japan studies, China studies, etc.). With this in mind, as Berndt notes at the end of her analysis, anime might actually work well in conjunction with media studies, reorienting what we think of as "area studies," whose central concern, as the name indicates, is "area." For anime's media-form insists that we engage with the questions of dislocation, of the problematic of this contemporary spatiality, forcing us to inquire about what an "area" is, where and how it operates, and the modes of existence such a spatiality may afford.

....

Stevie Suan is Assistant Professor at the Department of Global and Interdisciplinary Studies at Hosei University in Tokyo, Japan. He holds a doctorate in Manga Studies from the Graduate School of Manga Studies at Kyoto Seika University, and a Masters in Asian Studies from the University of Hawai'i at Mānoa.

....

Notes

1. Jaqueline Berndt, "Anime in Academia: Representative Object, Media Form, and Japanese Studies," *Arts,* 7, no. 4 (2018): 1–13.
2. Here Berndt builds on observations on Japan Studies by Michael K. Bourdaghs, "Review: Richard F. Calichman, Beyond Nation: Time, Writing, and Community in the Work of Abe Kôbô," *Critical Inquiry,* no. 44 (2018): 590–91.
3. Deborah Levitt, *The Animatic Apparatus: Animation, Vitality, and the Futures of the Image* (Winchester, UK: Zero Books, 2018), 59.
4. Levitt, *Animatic Apparatus,* 64.
5. Thomas Lamarre, *The Anime Machine: A Media Theory of Animation* (Minneapolis: University of Minnesota Press, 2009), 196.
6. Lamarre, *Anime Machine,* 201.
7. Lamarre, *Anime Machine,* 203.
8. Lamarre, *Anime Machine,* 206.
9. Marc Steinberg, *Anime's Media Mix: Franchising Toys and Characters in Japan* (Minneapolis: University of Minnesota Press, 2012), 6.
10. Hiroki Azuma, *Otaku: Japan's Database Animals,* trans. Jonathan E. Abel (Minneapolis: University of Minnesota Press, 2009).
11. Judith Butler, "Performative Acts and Gender Constitution: An Essay in Phenomenonology and Feminist Theory," *Theatre Journal* 40 (1988): 519–31.
12. Stevie Suan, "Anime's Performativity: Diversity through Conventionality in a Global Media-Form," *Animation: An Interdisciplinary Journal* 12 (2017): 62–79.
13. William Egginton, *How the World Became a Stage: Presence, Theatricality, and the Question of Modernity* (New York: SUNY Press, 2003).
14. Donald Crafton, *Shadow of a Mouse: Performance, Belief and World-Making in Animation* (Berkeley: University of California Press, 2013).

15. Stevie Suan, "Anime no 'kôisha': Animêshon ni okeru taigenteki/shûjiteki pafômansu ni yoru 'jiko' (Anime's Actors: Constituting 'Self-Hood' Through Embodied and Figurative Performance in Animation)," *Animêshon Kenkyû* 19, no. 1 (2017): 3–15.
16. Samuel Weber, *Theatricality as Medium* (New York: Fordham University Press, 2004), 388n6.
17. Weber, *Theatricality as Medium*, 185.
18. Ibid., 388n3.
19. Levitt, *Animatic Apparatus*, 59.
20. Lamarre, *Anime Machine*, 122.
21. Lamarre, *Anime Machine*, 134.
22. Lamarre, *Anime Machine*, 136.
23. Lamarre, *Anime Machine*, 141.
24. Lamarre, *Anime Machine*, 136.
25. Lamarre, *Anime Machine*, 139.
26. Paul Virilio, *Polar Inertia*, trans. Patrick Camiller (London: SAGE Publications, 2000), 85.
27. Michael Curtin, "Between State and Capital: Asia's Media Revolution in the Age of Neoliberal Globalization," *International Journal of Communication* 11 (2017): 1381.
28. Hye Jean Chung, "Media Heterotopia and Transnational Filmmaking: Mapping Real and Virtual Worlds," *Cinema Journal* 51 (2012): 90.
29. Chung, "Media Heterotopia and Transnational Filmmaking," 92.
30. Kukhee Choo, "Hyperbolic Nationalism: South Korea's Shadow Animation Industry," in *Mechademia 9: Origins*, ed. Frenchy Lunning, 144–62 (Minneapolis: University of Minnesota Press, 2015).
31. Doreen Massey, "A Global Sense of Place," in Massey, *Space, Place, and Gender* (Minneapolis: University of Minnesota Press, 1994).
32. Levitt, *Animatic Apparatus*, 65.
33. C. J. W.-L. Wee, "Imagining the Fractured East Asian Modern: Commonality and Difference in Mass-Cultural Production," *Criticism* 54, no. 2 (Spring 2012): 203.

(Re)Playing Anime

Building a Medium-specific Approach
to Gamelike Narratives

SELEN ÇALIK BEDIR

The ontological status of fictional characters has been a central issue in theoretical discourses on Japanese popular culture, especially in Japan. Since
the early 2000s, while Ôtsuka Eiji has attracted attention to the mortality of
semiotic bodies as a noteworthy particularity of manga and anime narratives,
some researchers following his lead have focused on characters' increasing
clinginess to life in recent works of Japanese popular culture. Being from
the second camp, in *Gêmuteki Riarizumu no Tanjô (The Birth of Gamelike Realism)*,[1] Hiroki Azuma extensively discusses light novels featuring characters
dying and coming back from death, or getting stuck in time loops to live the
same day or hour again and again. While Azuma's focus falls mainly on light
novels, not surprisingly this motif of "restart and repeat" is fairly common in
manga, anime, and even beyond Japanese popular culture, as it arguably finds
its roots in the coming of postmodernity. The weakening of widely accepted
social norms and values, which is usually acknowledged as a characteristic
of the postmodern age, seems to have deprived narratives of dominant directions for plot development, while the possibility of restarting a story after
it reaches an ending has been embraced as an efficient narrative strategy.
Today, in official sequels or prequels as well as in fan-made derivative works,
dead characters can be resurrected easily and their fates can be redrawn or
"replayed," which brings to mind the experience of playing games.

However, what seemingly emerges as a unifying quality, that is to say, a
"gamelikeness" that can be observed in contemporary narratives finding form
across media, goes against what is commonly acclaimed as a unique quality
that sets games apart from storytelling media. The distinguishing trait of
games is widely considered to be enabling repetitive interaction as opposed
to the developmental teleology of movies or novels. While Azuma does not
make it his goal to address medial differences, his discussion may provide
a new entrance point to reconsider the media that are compared to games,

specifically to reconsider anime, which incorporates audio elements like most video games, and possesses dynamic as well as static qualities. The question is, can we talk about an overarching similarity between contemporary media, that is, a gamelikeness, without disregarding media specificities? Can we use the concept to discover anime's specific take on gamelikeness?

Before addressing these questions, a definition of "medium" here is in order. In "Narration in Various Media" (2012), Marie-Laure Ryan lists three conceptual frameworks capturing three different aspects of media: semiotic, material-technological, and cultural.[2] Semiotically, for instance, anime is a pluricodal medium (combining visual and aural codes with language), which possesses both static and dynamic properties and produces narratives that extend over time and space. Anime's material-technological background (especially its reliance on the use of celluloid sheets, hand-drawn images and limited animation techniques) has particularized its narrative style further and even more visibly. On the other hand, anime has been in contact with digitalization for long enough to leave its material-technological limitations behind, at least, *potentially*. But instead, anime today chooses to embrace its material-technological heritage on a cultural level, by preserving cel animation style to a great extent even when computer graphics (CG) are heavily employed, and by keeping on picturing 2D worlds in a fashion that the audience has come to recognize. With the addition of its particular positioning on the cultural level, anime comes forward as a distinct medium.

In order to address media specificities, as the above application shows, at least the three aspects that Ryan covers should be taken into consideration, not only in connection with each other but also with time. To begin with, there is an intrinsic connection between a certain technology and the age in which it appears or stays in use. Moreover, the semiotic as well as the material-technological potential of a medium is always activated in relation to its cultural background, and to the predominant tastes or ways of thinking of the age. Thus, time leaves a significant mark on media, to the point that media specificities should be considered media *tendencies* that occur at specific periods in history, rather than a set of features that media display once and for all. These tendencies affect narrative potential as well, and so the following paragraphs will address the tendency in contemporary media to give form to a certain type of narrative displaying gamelikeness. Afterward, the focus will fall on individual media and finally on how exactly anime becomes gamelike and allows (re)play.

Origins of Gamelikeness and Conditions for (Re)Play

In *The Aesthetic of Play*, Brian Upton defines "play" as the "free movement within a system of constraints."[3] In the case of video games, this free movement corresponds to the moves of the gamers or the input they provide, while the system of constraints roughly corresponds to the rule system—provided by the game but interpreted by the gamer. Upton argues that the concept of play is applicable to games as well as to narrative media, taking place within the mind in the case of latter, as interpretive/anticipatory play. The information that media provide in their own ways (be it regarding storyworlds populated by characters or interactive spaces with few narrative elements) sets the parameters for the audience's interpretation of what is happening (the outcomes of their own actions or the characters') and what can possibly happen (the possible outcomes of future actions) as the process of play goes on. Upton's definition of play points toward a balance of predictability and unpredictability: while any system of constraints necessarily bring about the former, the freedom of movement that any form of play should provide requires the latter. However, as we will see, it is indeed a radical change in the nature of that balance that marks the core of gamelike narratives.

In *Dôbutsuka Suru Posutomodan: Otaku Kara Mita Nihon Shakai* (Otaku: Japan's database animals), Azuma spots the beginnings of the process that has brought about gamelike narratives in the early twentieth century, starting from 1914 to be more precise, and reaching full maturity at the end of the Cold War.[4] Basically, in Azuma's understanding, this period roughly covers the coming into being of postmodernity, and it is then the tendency to create gamelike narratives appears, due to significant changes in the environment that surrounds media. One of these changes is the unprecedented availability of a remarkably extensive pool of information to the public, made possible by the developments in information storage technologies and the internet. The appearance of this "database," as a byproduct of the connection that the internet keeps establishing between a constantly changing number of separate databases, has arguably changed the dynamics of narrative production and consumption. By revealing the most commonly used elements in the creation of narratives (from characters to settings), it has presented narratives in a new light, as a patchwork that can be taken apart. Moreover, as the disassembling process continues, it leaves us with what can be considered the building stones of narratives, rendered uniform, hence replaceable. These uniform units can be linked infinitely in different combinations if desired, allowing the characters to jump from setting to setting, setting off for new and great adventures.

However, surprisingly enough, it can be said that the seeds of this development were already present in the nineteenth-century realism. In *The Future of the Image*, Jacques Rancière states that a new type of artistic regime has appeared since the nineteenth century.[5] Under this "aesthetic regime," the arts have started to put together information of all sorts, and to feed the collective imagery as fast as they feed on it, now that mechanical presses and lithography allowed such circulation. Functioning already like an encyclopedia or an early form of database in a way, the arts of the nineteenth century proved to be in stark contrast with those organized by the principles of the previous "representative regime." The representative regime was a system that built a connection between what can be seen, said, and known; while dismissing the opposite (what *cannot* be seen, said, or known) from the arts. Therefore, it required the artists to carefully select the actions to be depicted according to their significance, and sufficiently clarify the causes and outcomes of these actions. As an example, Rancière brings into attention how Pierre Corneille diminished Tirésias's role when he rewrote Sophocles's *Oedipe* for stage in the seventeenth century. Corneille did this, according to Rancière's interpretation, for the oracles of Tirésias revealed too much regarding the plot development. In other words, in Corneille's thinking, it was necessary to limit the information shared with the audience, so that there would be no confusion about the causes and outcomes of whatever is happening on stage. Since the representative regime gave way to the aesthetic regime in the nineteenth century, the criteria for creating narratives have undergone striking changes. With the increasing accessibility of all sorts of information, in addition to famous historical figures or events, the ordinary lives and looks of lower-class people as well as background details such as mountains, fields, and even bugs have emerged as elements of significance in narration. In contrast to the preceding centuries, everything (any experience no matter how mundane) can be taken as a theme without a careful selection process since then. The hierarchy in the order of narration has vanished as well, making it possible, for instance, to jump to the topic of daily life right after war. However, there is a paradoxical side to this thematic/topical homogeneity. As they are narrated in the same manner, all sorts of actions and things get mixed up in a mass, losing the clear indications as to which matter more and how they are connected. Consequently, everything can be seen as the cause or the outcome of any other thing, meaning that causality (the relationship between cause and effect) receives a crippling blow.

Stephen Kern's extensive study, *A Cultural History of Causality* (2004), sheds more light upon the background of this phenomenon.[6] Kern tracks down the changes in novels featuring murder and its causes from the early nineteenth century to the beginning of the twenty-first, on the one hand, as he lines up scientific research carried out in various fields during the same period, on the other. Connecting the two strands, Kern's work attracts attention to the paradoxical impact of research on the understanding of causality. While scientific approaches to human behavior invalidate some widely held assumptions (such as the assumption that murderous intentions run in blood and haunt families over generations) with precise methods of analysis (such as the developments in genetics negating such long-term effects of a murderous gene), they also produce a web of uncertainty surrounding actions by revealing that a multitude of factors may apply in each case (as, in addition to genetics, countless sociological or psychological reasons can contribute to the making of a murderer). Therefore, in a sense, each discovery leads us further away from certainty (in the direction of probability), as it adds to the number of possible causes of an action and creates the awareness that there are always other potential causes beyond our understanding.

This summary of Kern's work seems to validate Rancière's theory, bringing to the fore the gradual transition from the nineteenth century to the twentieth and twenty-first centuries, as a deepening crisis of causality caused by the proliferation of information, instead of spotting a rupture in between these periods. Consequently, realist narratives appear to have an intrinsic connection with gamelike narratives, which may come as a surprise given that the latter is largely criticized for escapism. However, while some of the scientific discoveries that triggered the unraveling of causality can be traced back to the nineteenth century according to Kern's account (such as Gregor Mendel's establishing the foundations of modern genetics in 1865), it is only in the twentieth century that the implications of these discoveries could be grasped, and the disintegration of certain facts into a diversity of perspectives gained full visibility and form in modern literature. While Rancière's observation reveals that the first manifestations of the information proliferation's unsettling effect on causality in the arts appeared in the nineteenth century, at this early stage, when positivism and determinism were dominant philosophical theories, the shackles over the actions of characters (or their fate) remained tight. In fact, realist novels can be considered novels of limitations in many ways[7], but perhaps most obviously, of physical and social limitations. For instance, Jane Austen's characters are subject to laws of physics, but are constrained by more than that. In one of his caricatures for *The Guardian*, Tom Gauld lists five alternative endings for Austen's novels (Figure 1): leaving the heroine in embarrassment, in the care of a wealthy husband, in the care of an old aunt, in the grave after a fatal illness, or as a spinster.[8] Gauld's humor comes from the fact that it hits the right spot: these are endings one might indeed find in an Austen novel, reflecting how severely women's lives were constrained due to the overdetermining expectations of the age for proper actions and their outcomes. For the birth of contemporary gamelike narratives, as Azuma aptly emphasizes, another feature that marks postmodernity (along with the proliferation of information and as a result of it) needs to come into effect: the waning of widely accepted sociopolitical standards and the disappearing of their unifying force over narratives.

From a slightly different perspective, the same case can be taken as a good example of how the ties between characters and the environment surrounding them got blurred or even severed over time. In *Nihon kindai bungaku no kigen* (The origins of modern Japanese literature), Kôjin Karatani defines nineteenth-century literature as "the discovery of landscape," and claims that back then, by depicting the outside, its opposite, "the inside," was also created.[9] The narration that switches back and forth between painting the environment surrounding the characters and portraying the characters mentally as well as physically created a direct connection between the two. In the meantime, the outside became a binding force on the characters' actions and characteristics. Nineteenth-century realist novels made sure that the fates of the characters, such as the endings of Austen's novels, are drawn by the details of their physical and the social backgrounds, which are also described in detail. Written in the twentieth century but in a noticeably Dickensian manner, George Orwell's *Down and Out* captures this entwinement in narration vividly in the following paragraph:

> I am trying to describe the people in our quarter, not for the mere curiosity, but because they are all part of the story. Poverty is what I am writing about, and I had my first contact with poverty in this slum. The slum, with its dirt and its queer lives, was first an object-lesson in poverty, and then the background of my own experiences. It is for that reason that I try to give some idea of what life was like there.[10]

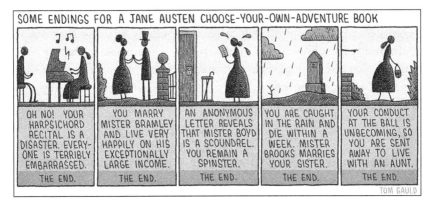

Figure 1. Tom Gauld, "Some Endings for a Jane Austen Choose-Your-Own-Adventure Cartoon," *The Guardian* (May 18, 2018). https://www.theguardian.com/books/picture /2018/may/18/tom-gauld-imagines-a-jane-austen-choose-your-own-adventure -cartoon (accessed April 19, 2019). Cartoon created by Tom Gauld.

As the passage indicates, the clues to understand a character were ideally scattered into the context and vice versa, meaning that neither characters nor contexts could be understood without thinking of them as a pair. It is possible to consider this state both a result of and a reaction to the proliferation of information itself. If the visibility of information caused a transference between characters and contexts, it also emerged as a means of securing them in each other's existence.

However, time has revealed that characters need not vanish in the absence of contextual cues once they are rendered recognizable enough. By employing well-known database elements in the making of characters, which is exactly how gamelike narratives are created, it is possible to discard the need for any details regarding these fictional beings that the "outside" environment could provide. In other words, if the potential of collective imagery is fully embraced in the production and consumption of narratives, characters do not have to show compatibility with their surroundings or abide by their rules. This is also how gamelike narratives are imbued with randomness on the other hand, which indeed should be considered a requirement for the type of narratives in question, for they are constantly created in their own image, by piecing together the elements with which the audience is more than familiar.

This being the case, the increasing visibility of narrative elements and the decreasing causality in line with it create a balance of opposites: extreme predictability and extreme unpredictability. Differing from before in intensity, this combination allows for characters to gain freedom from their contexts, or mobility. Play is always possible once there is a balance, as Upton suggests, of predictability and unpredictability. But (re)playing gamelike narratives (that is, taking characters out of their contexts and imagining them in alternative scenarios) emerges as an option only when the visibility of all too many possibilities undermine building a reliable sense of causality.

Underplaying Causality in Worlds with and without Limits

In *Adventure, Mystery, and Romance,* John G. Cawelti draws attention to a similar point, by claiming that "[w]e might loosely distinguish between formula stories and their 'serious' counterparts on the ground that the latter tend toward some kind of encounter with our sense of the limitations of reality, while formulas embody moral fantasies of a world more exciting, more fulfilling, or more benevolent than the one we inhabit."[11] In other words, "mimetic" narratives (roughly overlapping with the arts) opt for a more pronounced sense of limitation in Cawelti's understanding, while formulaic or popular narratives depict more loosely organized worlds (allowing for miracles) inhabited by larger than life characters. In addition, though, Cawelti makes it clear that he refrains from building an unsurmountable barrier between the two categories by stating that breaches of border into both directions are not only possible but also necessary to an extent. Even by this brief quote, it is apparent that Cawelti presents a strong argument that covers a wide ground, especially in that it attracts attention to the nature of the context (storyworlds) in narratives.

However, taking up Cawelti's argument in the scope of this article calls for two additional points. The author attracts attention to the permeability of the border he comes up with, and to the fluidity of his concept of "formula," defined as "a combination or synthesis of a number of specific cultural conventions with a more universal story form or archetype,"[12] which establishes its core in repetition and evolves at the same time. Nevertheless, it can still be argued that separating narratives along this axis (of mimetic versus formulaic) proves problematic. While seeking a difference along this axis, the full effects of the transformation in the media environment that applies not only to popular narratives but also to the arts can go unnoticed. To put it clearly, this separation runs the risk of missing the tendency to obfuscate causality observed in contemporary media (including the arts) in general.

Along with this overarching tendency, the particularities of media which shape narratives on a micro level seems to go unnoticed as well. While the extreme visibility of narrative elements blurs the causal connections between them and thus arouses unpredictability, paradoxically it does also present an extreme predictability, now that character, plotline, and setting *types* are revealed, which bring to mind alternatives for each element. Plus, characters' ever present potential for triumph threatens to bore the audience, unless the path leading to the foreseeable ending is filled with surprises. To put it differently, as the endings can always be rewritten until the point of satisfaction, it becomes the *how* that attracts the audience rather than *where* the characters end up. While creating ambiguity (for introducing an element of surprise) seems to be a necessity for contemporary media in general, a brief intermedial comparison will reveal that there are individualized ways of creating ambiguity.

Without delving into medium specificities, Cawelti takes up the James Bond series as an example among many others to reveal the complex entanglement of mimetic and formulaic elements in any given narrative. James Bond's world is depicted closely to the one that the audience inhabits, and to his world as well the laws of physics seem to apply. Consequently, the audience can take an educated guess as to what is physically possible in this world, and what kind of outcomes should follow certain actions. His world functioning similarly to the real world, Bond's fall from a steep cliff should prove fatal or at least injurious, for he should also be subject to gravity. Yet, those who are familiar with this fictional character know that concerns over Bond's health are largely unnecessary thanks to his exceptional physical skills, wits, and high-tech equipment. The "exceptional" here borders on "supernatural" for the frequency it is invoked, and for its high rate of success. Bond might also get lucky and survive his fall from a steep cliff, just like sheer luck may save anyone from a terrible disaster in the real world too. Still, the continuity in Bond's lucky streak diverges from real life occurrences as well, indicating once again that we might be following the adventures of a supernatural being rather than a normal person whose life is constrained by an uncountable set of factors. In short, Bond can engage in actions with unpredictable outcomes, despite the fact that he lives in a world that seems to function in close proximity to ours, and defy causality thanks to his exceptional characteristics.

Animations, obviously, do not have to depict worlds that resemble the one in which their audiences live. Nevertheless, aiming for a close mimicry of cinematic conventions, Disney works resort to drawings and modeling that seem to follow movement and "capture" the minute details in the flow of action just like the cinematic camera does. Here, movement develops over time in relation to space and brings about a change in the position of the moving object. Following the action as it leads to a new state of things emphasizes causality. However, Disney does not simply end up importing the physics of the real world. Instead, it creates "hyperrealism" by combining the potential of animation with cinematic conventions: as it incorporates the laws of physics in animation on the one hand, it also makes it clear that the characters depicted are fictional beings that a camera cannot capture. It is a signature move of Disney to grant characters magical qualities or exceptional physical forms that allow them to defy physics. Disney makes its characters magical, exceptional, or both; therefore, even if they are in a (not necessarily realistically depicted but consistent thus) predictable environment, their actions do not necessarily produce expected results. After falling from steep cliffs, it is possible that these characters unexpectedly get suspended in the air or bounce off the ground, creating a comical effect. But if they do create a comical effect, it is exactly because gravity *exists* in Disney worlds: audience expectations hit a brick wall, as physics do not apply to some characters despite its pronounced presence. In the meantime, characters' individual configurations infinitely diversify how these exceptional characters can defy the limits of their worlds and how their adventures will unravel.

Despite the flatness of their looks, 2D animations can also opt for building worlds where real world physics is expected to be at work. Moreover, this capacity is present even in limited animation. Even when the movement is not drawn (in contrast to full animation) but drawings are moved instead, it is possible in this sort of animation to stabilize the effects of continuing movement on space via montage. As long as the phases of change are revealed consistently, one can talk about the presence of some rules that organize actions and their outcomes. Struggling with budgetary constraints during the medium's birth, anime creators had to push this potential in limited animation, and relied heavily on the *implication* of movement born out of the combination of still images with sound. However, this technique comes with a risk. If the combination of still images with sound is extended for too long over time, as it indefinitely delays the outcomes of actions despite the implication of movement, it can give the impression that there are inconsistencies in the storyworld that real world physics cannot account for.

This latent risk reveals itself perhaps most dramatically when it is not embraced openly. For example, *Monster*, a seinen series with thriller elements (first appearing as manga in 1994, followed by a novel, anime series, and live action), mostly goes for dramatic coincidences and timely revelations of omitted details in narration to surprise the audience, reserving the blatantly supernatural for only one character even though not entirely wiping it off the table. *Monster* can be considered a realistic title for emphasizing the limitations on the all-too-human protagonist, how his fate is irreversibly shaped by the choices he makes in certain points of his life, by his profession, by his position against the law. In the anime as well, the emphasis on Dr. Tenma's limitations as a human being, or his lack of power to change physically and otherwise disadvantageous situations at will, preserves its centrality. Therefore, when Tenma is given quite a beating with a billiards cue in the episode 15, it builds the expectation that he will get severely injured after being struck repeatedly in the face with a stick. However, at one point, as the tormentor gets carried away in his accusatory speech and deals consecutive blows on Tenma's face over two shots, the third shot shows only a few faint scratches on the characters forehead and cheeks. In this scene, while repeated movement extends over time in combination with the character's speech, it brings us close to a crisis of causality. As the beating does not seem to cause any changes on Tenma's condition, the limits of what the protagonist can do are pushed beyond the audience's predictions, and for a brief period of time, up until the injurious effects of the heavy beating finally appear on the protagonist's face following a short delay, it appears possible that Tenma is in possession of supernatural powers.

The beating scene in *Monster* eventually produces the expected results and reaffirms its adherence to a set of limitations creating a reliable sense of causality in the depicted storyworld. However, contemporary shônen anime displaying more pronounced "gamelike" qualities unleash this very potential of limited animation to annul limits in order to allow for (re)play. Differing from Disney works, contemporary anime see no problem in downplaying the connections between actions, the contexts they take place in, and their outcomes; in fact, it acknowledges this move as a valid narrative option. Even when a high degree of verisimilitude is attained through the technique of rotoscope, which can present the real world as the setting of animetic action, contemporary anime mostly do not operate on the logic that movement over time should present changes in the positioning of the moving object in its surrounding environment. In short, a sort of suspendable environment is created, which has no consistent connection with and check upon actions in general.

This, we can say, is the construction of worlds with no limits, allowing any character (any single body, however unlikely) to defy predictions and become a superhero, rather than granting some characters the exceptional qualities to beat the physics of the world around them. While the potential to create limitless worlds in anime was awakened in part by budgetary requirement, it comes to light in accordance with the more generally observed waning of causality as a guiding principle in the making of narratives, getting more and more obviously reflected in the plot as well.

One of the most famous titles that embrace limitlessness as the guiding condition in narration is definitely *Dragon Ball Z* (based on the latter 325 chapters of the *Dragon Ball* manga, the chapters published between 1988 and 1995). During the fights taking place throughout the series, certain actions (i.e., attacks) are constantly assigned numerical values. However, despite the precision, these numbers are not generally presented in relation to a full scale of values, and even if they are, the actions of the characters do not come to a halt upon reaching the maximum and minimum points indicated. When such numerical limits are breached, the erratic occurrence is often explained as a triumph of the will or emotions, which presents narrative inconsistencies as manifestations of the incalculable human potential and renders them plotwise acceptable. Through repetition, the ambiguity concerning the actual limits of actions becomes a natural trait of narration.

While an ambiguity concerning causality is exactly what is necessary to imagine familiar characters in "new" (or rather recycled) scenarios, some shônen titles such as *Dragon Ball Z* openly embrace the strategy of creating worlds where the notion of limitation itself holds no water. Parodying the shônen genre itself, *One Punch Man* is even more willing to take this path, revealing from the start that the only limit that functions is that the protagonist needs to prevail no matter what. Moreover, in *One Punch Man*, it is also absolutely clear from the title that the protagonist has only one move. Such an overdetermined plot is bound to be boring unless somehow a space of ambiguity is created. In this particular series, even though there is an absolute limit indicated—namely, the one and only punch—it turns out that this limit itself can be disintegrated into a multitude by elaborating on the basically infinite qualities that a punch may display: In the final fight of the first season, the protagonist beats his rival with regenerative powers with the use of "serious" one punch and "consecutive" one punch. Once limits are erased or lose function through such disintegration, irreconcilable elements can be brought together. In this way, *One Punch Man*, just like the shônen series it parodies, evokes interest in the audience as to *how* victory will be gained (instead of *if* victory will be gained). In the meanwhile, the paradox that the shônen hero can do anything in a perfectly decided plot is exaggerated to the maximum for comic effect.

Encouraging (Re)play in Media-Specific Ways

If gamelikeness finds fertile ground in limitless worlds, it may seem counter-productive for gamelike narratives to take up videogames (which operate on computerized systems of limitations) as a trope. However, not only is gaming culture quite often invoked in anime, manga. and light novels, but there is also an increasing number of titles that are directly about adventures taking place in online gameworlds. Among those, *.hack* (anime series and game first appearing in 2002, followed by light novels and manga) can be listed as one of the earliest, while *Log Horizon* (*Rogu Horaizun*, originally light novels, published first in 2011, followed by manga and anime series), *Accel World* (*Akuseru Waârudo*, originally a light novel series published first in 2010, followed by manga, anime, and games) and *Sword Art Online* (*Sôdo Âto Onrain*, first appearing as a light novel series in 2009, followed by manga, anime, and game series) are only some of the more recent and quite popular titles. As they mimic the aesthetics of videogames and videogame interfaces, these titles also reveal that in fact gamelike narratives quite organically accommodate the depiction of any strict system to their benefit. Following the same pattern described in the previous section (as in *Dragon Ball Z* and *One Punch Man*), they emphasize the existence of a system of limits quite deliberately, *only for the hero to defy it at an unforeseeable moment to great affective impact.* One of the best examples of the case would be the protagonist's coming back to life after seeing the "game over" screen in *Sword Art Online*.

As exemplified in this instance, the game system is introduced as a trope and invoked in such titles to keep the audience on their toes, waiting for the inevitable-yet-unpredictable to strike in storyworlds where anything can happen. Ironically, however, such intense unpredictability undermines the sense of accomplishment for the gamer in videogames. As long as there are goals in a game (such as victory or completion), some actions are bound to be more beneficial than others, and gamers need to build an idea regarding the possible consequences of their in-game actions so that they can make mean-ingful (i.e., not random) decisions leading to their goals. Therefore, game interfaces drop causal clues for the gamers, and game systems simulate certain outcomes for the set of actions they enable (which also becomes a causal cue in itself). While causality is not *always* pronounced to the utmost extreme in games either,[13] the nature of gamelike narratives is visibly marked by a crisis of causality and ambiguity from birth. In other words, the way that games enable play is fundamentally different from the way gamelike narratives enable (re)play, in that the latter purposefully weaken causal connections to allow the audience to explore alternative routes for plot development.

Among gamelike narratives, further particularities in the manifestation of ambiguity across media can be unearthed through a comparison between manga and anime. The *Sword Art Online* manga, for instance, can be considered a typical example of its kind for possessing some widely discussed manga-esque elements. To begin with, it displays a conspicuous use of speed lines, which play a big role in the narrative style of contemporary manga as Scott McCloud points out,[14] prominent to the extent that it quite often blocks the setting entirely, putting the characters, especially their faces in the center of attention. In fact, McCloud claims that manga has effective ways of conveying emotions, one of them being such focus on characters in front of abstracted background. Similarly, though Itô Gô points out mainly in relation to shôjo manga,[15] the uneven sizes and the overlapping placement or fusion of panels can be found in many recent manga like *Sword Art Online*. Instead of breaking the movement into a series of traceable steps, this style seems to shatter it into pieces that orbit around the characters. Movement gets pushed to the background, not only because of this style of paneling but also because of the contents of the panels, for the perspectives of the characters along with the mental images, they end up occupying the same space with the depiction of movement. As this jumbling of external and internal perspectives is aligned with characters' inner voices quite often, their will and emotions seem to stand out as the guiding force of narrative. This guiding force, however, is erratic by nature, and the limits of what can be done in manga worlds remain beyond the deduction skills of the readers.

Nevertheless, it may be argued that such masking of the action is taken to exist on the representational level only; in other words, the readers must acknowledge that the action takes place in the storyworld although its depiction is omitted for the sake of convenience. Consequently, it can be surmised that the flow of action implied by the medium is sorted out in the minds of the readers, just like the gaps between panels are supposed to be filled out in the mind.

In the case of anime, on the other hand, the blocked or omitted action *can* take place right before the audience's eyes, as the medium has dynamic properties in contrast with manga. However, exactly because anime *opts for not doing so*, it does present us with the same type of limitless worlds that manga also creates. The animating style that anime tends to maintain, despite the availability and ease in the use of CG, partially animates manga panels over time rather than filling up the gap between selected panels with movement. By keeping the animation of drawings at the minimum, it implies the presence of movement, relying, just like manga, on the power of imagination. However, as a dynamic spatiotemporal medium, anime has a different relationship with temporality: As discussed previously, if the medium extends minimized or partial movement for a long period of time without revealing any outcome, it risks producing a crisis of action. In *The Anime Machine*, Thomas Lamarre discusses such occasions in relation to film theory and particularly to Gilles Deleuze's concept of the "time-image." Lamarre aptly points out that the animetic time-image combines the crisis of action with a vivid display of emotions, pushing characters' troubled "souls" to the surface of the screen in a sense.[16]

Approaching the effects of this particular form of time-image within the framework of gamelikeness discussed so far in this article, we can say that its frequent emergence in action scenes produces spaces of ambiguity where the audience:

does not see exactly what happens,

cannot guess exactly what will happen due to the insufficiency of visual elements or their arrhythmical unraveling (which gets in the way of building or applying causal connections),

yet can sense (through the audio-visual display of emotions taking up the space for representation of movement in combination with sound effects) that something of great physical and emotional impact takes place.

Tracing the development of action is not a priority in anime, although that might be the expectation. In light of the previous discussion, tracing the development of action in gamelike narratives might be considered even irrelevant, in the sense that actions' outcomes (hence plot development) are decided by unpredictable factors or randomly. Shônen anime in particular tends to visualize and verbalize emotions instead of action, which gives the audience a basis to interpret what is happening (as intense untraceable action and ensuing emotional crisis), while emotions appear (by preceding actions' outcomes and seemingly effecting them) as the guiding force of the depicted worlds. This arrangement proves an efficient way of inviting ambiguity while bypassing the need to come up with new (pseudo-)explanations for each time there is a breach of limits in the storyworlds. As emotions are inestimable in nature, presenting emotions as the operating principle of a universe eradicates the need for finding an excuse for any overdue revelation of exceptional characteristics or previously unknown factors that updates our understanding of the environment. (Re)playing anime rests on knowing that anything can happen in such (emotionally organized) limitless worlds where every character is a potential hero, or more specifically within the playspaces of ambiguity that the medium creates in its own way, with its own tools, at a given time, and recombining salvageable narrative elements in new ways if desired. (Re)playing anime is consciously using the medium-specific manifestations of ambiguity to recreate alternative plot developments and endings in this age of information imposing an extreme predictability on narratives.

....

Selen Çalık Bedir received her BA in English Language and Literature from Bogaziçi University (2008) and her MA in Comparative Literature from Istanbul Bilgi University (2010) in Turkey. From 2012 to 2017, she studied in Japan on a MEXT grant. After spending one year as a research student at Kyoto University (2012-13), she entered the PhD program in Manga Studies at Kyoto Seika University (2013). Selen currently works as an assistant professor at Beykoz University.

....

Notes

1. Azuma Hiroki, *Gemuteki riarizumu no tanjô: Dôbutsuka suru posutomodan 2* (Tokyo: Kodansha, 2007).
2. Marie-Laure Ryan, "Narration in Various Media," in the *Living Handbook of Narratology*, ed. Peter Hühn et. al (Hamburg: Hamburg University). http://www.lhn.uni-hamburg.de/article/narration-various-media (accessed April 19, 2019).
3. Brian Upton, *The Aesthetics of Play* (Cambridge, MA: The MIT Press, 2015), 15.
4. Azuma Hiroki, *Dôbutsuka suru posutomodan: Otaku kara mita Nihon shakai* (Tokyo: Kôdansha, 2001), translated by Jonathan E. Abel and Shion Kono as *Otaku: Japan's Database Animals* (Minneapolis: University of Minnesota Press, 2009).

5. Jacque Rancière, *Le Destin des Images* (Paris: Éd. La Fabrique, 2003), translated by Gregory Elliott as *The Future of the Image* (London: Verso, 2007).

6. Stephen Kern, *A Cultural History of Causality: Science, Murder Novels, and Systems of Thought* (Princeton: Princeton University Press, 2004).

7. Boris Groys, "Towards the New Realism," *E-flux Journal* 77 (November 2016), http://www.e-flux.com/journal/77/77109/towards-the-new-realism/ (accessed January 5, 2017).

8. Tom Gauld, "Some Endings for a Jane Austen Choose-Your-Own-Adventure Cartoon," *The Guardian* (May 18, 2018), https://www.theguardian.com/books /picture/2018/may/18/tom-gauld-imagines-a-jane-austen-choose-your-own -adventure-cartoon (accessed April 19, 2019).

9. Karatani Kôjin, *Nihon kindai bungaku no kigen* (Tokyo: Kôdansha, 1980), translated by Brett de Bary as *The Origins of Modern Japanese Literature* (Durham: Duke University Press, 1993).

10. George Orwell, *Down and Out in Paris and London* (London: Penguin, 1940), 5.

11. John G. Cawelti, *Adventure, Mystery, and Romance: Formula Stories as Art and Popular Culture* (Chicago: University of Chicago Press, 1976), 38.

12. Cawelti, *Adventure, Mystery, and Romance*, 6.

13. See Selen Çalık, *"Playing" Anime: A Comparative Media-Theoretical Approach to Anime as a Specific Medium*, PhD diss., Kyoto Seika University, 2017, 127–32.

14. Scott McCloud, "Understanding Manga," *Wizard Magazine* (April 1996), 44–48.

15. Itô Gô, *Tezuka izu deddo: Hirakareta hyôgenron e* (Tokyo: NTT shuppan, 2005).

16. Thomas Lamarre, *The Anime Machine: A Media Theory of Animation* (Minneapolis: University of Minnesota Press, 2009), chap. 15.

Material Conditions and Semiotic Affordances

Natsume Fusanosuke's Many Fascinations with the Lines of Manga

LUKAS R. A. WILDE

Comics and manga, in all their generic and cultural variations, are typically considered *multimodal* forms of expressions. Although many wordless variants exist, they typically combine written and pictorial modes of expression to represent worlds, as well as characters and sequences of events located within these worlds. The specificity and distinctiveness of *pictoriality*, however—of "being an image"—remains extremely hard to define. Since pictoriality is often treated as a material given, at core "untranslatable" in other semiotic modes such as the written language, it should come as no surprise that many picture theories dissociate themselves from semiotics as clearly as possible. James Elkins's highly insightful study *On Pictures and the Words that Fail Them* (1998), for instance, is opened up by the following words:

> This book might well have been titled *The Antisemiotic*, since much of what I have to say here runs against the tendency to interpret pictures as systems of signs, or—in the looser but more prevalent formula—as examples of visual language.[1]

In striking contrast, it has been argued within Japanese manga discourse—by practitioners as well as by theorists, maybe most prominently by Ôtsuka Eiji— that the pictures of manga should *not* be considered pictures at all but rather a form of "hieroglyphics" or a "semiotic code."[2] Since around the mid-1990s, a strand of theory became visible that is now called *manga hyôgenron*. It is usually translated as "theories of manga expression," understood in a rather narrow sense as "stylistics" or "aesthetics" of manga. Nearly at the same time when Scott McCloud published *Understanding Comics* (1993), in which he separated any "contents" of comics from their "form," Natsume Fusanosuke and Takekuma Kentarô expressed a similar interest with *Manga no yomikata* (How to read manga, 1995).[3] Here, they developed fundamental theories, taxonomies, and typologies of basic manga elements such as speed and impact lines, pictograms *(kei'yu)*, sound words, speech balloons, background patterns, and so on. Within this line of discourse, highly sophisticated semiotic theories have since been developed that focus on formal functions, internal structures, and the meaning of discrete elements within the medium. On the first glance, our everyday understanding of comics as, say, "sequential images," should apply to Natsume's conception of manga as well:

> At least the contemporary manga (including the one-panel-manga) is composed in the format of frames *[koma]* with contents of pictures *[e]*. To Japanese people today, manga is a particular form of expression *[hyôgen]* based mostly on pictures included in consecutive frames. If one of both elements disappears, no manga emerges.[4]

Why, then, is Natsume insisting that we should not mistake the "manga expressions" *(manga hyôgen)* for anything but "an accumulation of conventions"?[5] Why, for that matter, does his collaborator Takekuma Kentarô state that "any manga-frame does not merely contain 'pictures and letters,' but actually various structures of accumulated, heterogeneous signs *[kigô]*."[6] Many manga theorists, in fact, build their conceptions not at all on the idea of a verbal/visual-divide but rather on an emphasis on "line-pictures" *(senga)* with clear "outline borders" and "demarcations" *(rinkaku, sakaime,* or *kyôkai-sen)*:[7] "The line is the most important element for the emergence of pictures."[8] What, then, are the very material conditions at the core of the Japanese media mix, and in what way can they be addressed as semiotic "affordances" that *might* cross a threshold toward pictoriality?[9]

I argue that Natsume's "emergence" of pictoriality in manga constitutes in fact not one but two threshold conditions and that these must be addressed independently from each other, one way or the other; at least, if we are to make sense of the author's manyfold "fascinations" or "attractions" *(miryoku)* that "capitalize on the ambiguity of the line."[10] And, if Natsume is right, the same "primordial attraction of the line" that we can observe with respect to certain visual puns must also be taken into account in most (if not all) works of the medium.[11] Natsume's overall fascination rests in his amazement of how it is possible that a mere "aggregation of lines" can "force" recipients to recognize representations of human beings, as well as of emotions.[12] However, everything we seem to recognize with such ease can just as easily turn out to be a deception, often exploited for surprising and comical effects. Natusume followed this thought in many later publications. I draw on *Manga wa naze omoshiroi no ka: Sono hyôgen to bunpô* (What makes manga fascinating? On expressions and grammar, 1997), which is itself based on a series of broadcastings on NHK's educational television format *Ningen daigaku* (The university of humanity) from July 1996 on.

In the following article, I trace some of the key arguments in Natsume's manga theory by relating them to cognitive semiotics and transmedial narratology. I would like to show that we can—and must—distinguish at least two levels of pictorial meaning present in the line-pictures of most (if not all) manga: on the one hand, the perceptual or phenomenological sensation of seeing three-dimensional objects "in" two-dimensional surfaces (part 1). On the other hand, however, we can usually infer some *referential meaning* from this experience. Manga not only present pictorial substitute stimuli but also re-present characters, objects, or scenes as part of an absent *storyworld* or a *diegesis* (part 2). As such, the respective lines refer to a space-time location different from the site of the actual perceptual experience. If such worlds are thought of as possible, perceptual "lifeworlds," I would like to discuss to what extent these two levels can indeed be "mapped" onto each other: to what respect is a picture object in *representational correspondence* to its referential meaning (part 3)? In subsequent paragraphs, I come full circle by addressing a related peculiarity of Natsume's theory, his original account of manga-specific pictograms (*kei'yu* and *man'pu*) such as sweat beads or light bulbs (part 4). While these are usually treated as distinct cases from "regular" pictures in manga, it will be possible to show that they are indeed closely related to the two thresholds under discussion. In a short conclusion (part 5), I summarize how the *modality* and the *mediality* of pictorial signs in manga could be conceptually distinguished from and related to each other, and what this means for our understanding of manga as media.

1. Pictoriality and the Experience of Picture Objects

Let us have look at Natsume's first ambiguity, his first source of fascination:

> A line, in the stage before it is about to signify [*arawasu*] anything, has the primordial attraction to become a snake as well as a rope. The same kind of attraction can be found within manga.[13]

Looking at works of Sugiura Shigeru, a manga artist of the 1930s who became quite famous after the war for his surreal gags, Natsume concedes that his line drawings possess "many indeterminate forms."[14] They present geometrical, often amorphous bodies and spatial objects that, more often than not, defy figurative signification beyond the lines on paper that they indeed are. Another artist under discussion is Tanioka Yasuji (famous in the 1970s), notorious for his outrageous, crude gags and his explosive "in-your-face" humor. His characters were composed of mere sketches, simplest outline-shapes, and extreme reductions. Sometimes, we only get to see a semicircle and some dots within a frame that can only later be recognized as "some kind of human face" (in very skewed proportions) by looking at subsequent frames. Tanioka also plays with uncertainties whether his lines demark physical bodies in the first place, or are merely intended to be a part of speech bubbles, speed lines, or frame demarcations. What all these examples show, following Natsume, is that some lines can be "interesting," even when "we cannot yet have any certain awareness what subject [taishô] has been drawn."[15] The subsequent riddle that haunts the author throughout his writings is what exactly happens "when pictures are born out of lines"?[16]

Picture theory might primarily be conceived as a general (and mostly inclusive) theoretical framework that allows viewers to regard pictures prototypically as signs close to perception, as Klaus Sachs-Hombach has suggested.[17] Seeing something "in" a picture involves certain perceptual competences that are—up to a point—likewise employed in the interaction with "regular" kinds of objects. The term "seeing-in" was coined by Richard Wollheim.[18] To make the distinction to linguistic signs (whose content can only ever be mentally present) more prominent, phenomenological and perceptual picture theories prefer the term "picture objects" over "picture contents."[19] We recognize or experience picture objects "in" specific forms of materiality (the latter sometimes called the "picture vehicle," or the "picture thing").[20] According to Umberto Eco's later conception, prototypical pictures can then be said to provide "surrogate stimuli" of perception.[21] Elsewhere, I have discussed in more detail to what extent this model can be applied to our most restricted "picture objects," emoticons, kaomoji, and emoji.[22] No explicit knowledge of a code is needed—when and if a certain iconic threshold is sufficiently exceeded by the visual stimuli. This perceptual situation is called "alpha mode" by Eco.[23] It is explicitly distinguished from "beta mode," in which the same threshold is not sufficiently exceeded. Hence, when not enough relevant stimuli are provided, the line can just as well "become" a rope as a snake—or an unspecified number of additional things.

What, then, about all the highly stylized and conventionalized manga representations that certainly look nothing like stimuli within the real world? Semiotician Börries Blanke makes a helpful distinction between *iconic codes* on the one hand (which we have to learn beforehand, or to infer in order to "see" the picture objects accordingly) and *iconic conventions* on the other.[24] Iconic conventions can be observed with regards to pictorial representations that are still well within mode alpha (above the iconic threshold), but with regard to which a *specific* pictorial actualization is nevertheless repeatedly preferred. Neil Cohn's recent descriptions of a "Japanese Visual Language" could best be seen as an attempt to describe exactly such iconic conventions, understood now as standardized patterns of representation that nevertheless require no prior knowledge or special training for their recognition (but certainly for their production).[25] The interesting examples discussed by Natsume, however, are not only nowhere close to prototypical pictures such as photographs, but also—just like droodles or "picture riddles," which they actually *are*—intentionally below that alpha-level of iconicity. They border on iconic codes.

The fact that neither *explicit* knowledge nor any kind of guesses to communicative intentions are necessary to see something "in" pictures above the first threshold provides a solid explanation for Natsume's astonishment that it is possible to *surprise oneself* by drawing a droodle. A child, applying lines on a paper, might suddenly realize it has created the drawing of a human face, without any prior intentions to do so. This is, maybe, the core of the "fascination" or "attraction" of the line, which seems to be able to "dictate meanings." Natsume describes this as the experience of a sudden "leap of the consciousness" if we cannot help to (suddenly) recognize a line as a depicted object.[26] We could rephrase this now: In these cases, the threshold of iconic categorization has been crossed—but just barely.

2. Pictoriality and the Referential Meaning of Represented Storyworlds

Natsume's second ambiguity of the line is something completely different. It is based on a subversion of the principle of identity that is established *between* the many frames of a work—and thus much more comic- or manga-specific. Natsume now references artists such as Taigâ Tateishi (Tateishi Kôichi) who produced short gag strips during the 1970s. Taigâ Tateishi's strips often feature seven panels that built up toward a specific "visual punch line," mostly without any texts at all. Usually, the whole "point" of his strips is a surprising metamorphosis or transformation, what Paul Wells discussed in detail as "visual puns" for animated film.[27] A line representing a rope transforms into waving lines when it is rotated in the following panel, only to morph into a branch of soybeans in the next. In other strips, a horizon line suddenly becomes a physical edge or a razor-sharp string that cuts objects into half. Natsume rightly observes that these kind of "deceiving pictures" rest on the regular functions of the frame-arrangements (the *koma-wari*) and the gutter between frames (the *mahaku*).[28] The frame-arrangement is "a gridline that is visible to the eye, but in fact it must be understood as the abstract possibility of manga's spatial and temporal articulation."[29] Internationally, the process by which recipients synthesize the segmented (or articulated) contents of various panel in order to inferentially construct a coherent whole is called *closure*.

The domain where this "whole" is situated is, of course, the *diegesis*, or the *storyworld* of the comic, which is understood as "a world populated by individuated existents."[30] The prerequisite of such a world clearly differentiates comics and manga from other kinds of pictorial signs, such as emoticons, emoji, or pictograms, even though the first threshold is the same. Media and comics scholar Stephan Packard dedicated many thoughts on the matter that "the (many) narrative comics are those that typically represent individuated objects, in the sense of a minimal realism of objects within an extensional world."[31] A strong conceptual connection between a given medium's *narrativity* and its faculty to represent individuated entities is a presupposition of Natsume's as well:

> That a desk is consistently a desk, a cloud a cloud, and a person consistently that same person, this "reality-likeness" [*genjitsu-rashisa*] is the preamble for any story. By this craft, the original ambiguity of the line is suppressed, for everything is then drawn in such a way that it is determined by that impression of reality.[32]

It is exactly this narrative principle of identity that gag manga-artists such as Taigâ Tateishi break with, in order to surprise with visual puns and magical transformations: "One could say that this author was conceptually obsessed by the question what drawn line-shapes could become."[33] The subsequent narratological conundrums have been extensively discussed in "Western" (European and North-American) comic book theories as well, for instance by Ole Frahm or Steven Surdiacourt—incidentally with regard to "line gags" very similar to Taigâ Tateishi's, as George Herriman's *Krazy Kat* strips.[34] There, too, a line can first represent a horizon, only to be physically "cut" by the protagonist's scissors later. Terminologically, it might be problematic to speak of "reference" in all these cases, since they are clearly fictional. We might thus prefer the term *referential meaning*, widely used in film studies and proposed by Jan-Noël Thon for a transmedial application.[35] The referential meaning of a given work might be conceptualized as the sum of all the facts that "are the case" within the work's storyworld. It can be further divided up in locally represented situations that are part of a globally represented (or merely implied) storyworld. The latter is thus often understood as a "basic facts domain."[36]

A sharp distinction from the plane of picture objects (that we see "in" pictures) remains necessary. A storyworld could best be considered as a normative abstraction of (or rather *about*) actual reception processes, identical neither with individual mental representations nor with the medial representations on which the reception is based. It is thus a mere approximation, sometimes taken as "prescribed" or "mandated imaginations."[37] In a concise way, Jan-Noël Thon puts it like this: "[S]toryworlds are what recipients *should* imagine based on narrative representations, but they do not exist independently of these imaginations, and recipients are, of course, quite free to imagine something entirely different."[38] To make this somewhat less abstract: If we decide to imagine, for instance, that speedlines represent a character having "floating strings attached to his or her body," this will certainly be a private venture. It is clear that speed lines are meant to represent *that something is moving*—anyone versed in the respective manga conventions would understand it as a prompt to imagine just that. A represented situation (as part of a storyworld) can then, by definition, not be conflated with what we phenomenologically see "in" a picture. This is a decisively private experience or, in the words of Wollheim, it is "a perceptual, more narrowly a visual, phenomenon."[39] To get back to Natsume and his many examples: we would miss the whole "point" of all these visual puns if we would *not* presuppose referential situations within coherent storyworlds "behind" or "beyond" what we see in single frames. Natsume's second "fascination" rests precisely on this assumption (and its subversion).

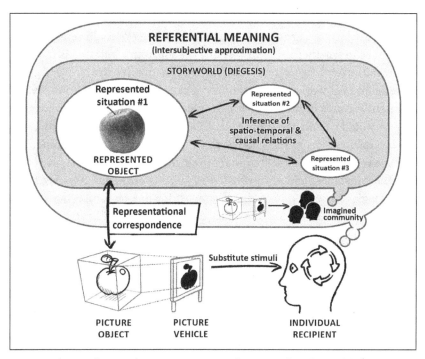

Figure 1. Planes of pictorial meaning in manga. Illustration by Kilian Wilde (www .wilde-grafik.com), used with permission.

Figure 1 serves as a schematic illustration for the distinction between both planes, between picture objects and their referential meaning. Not only the material carrier but also the pictorial substitute stimuli are still on the side of the means of representation—and not on the side of the represented situations (or the represented objects within them). Since the latter are located within a work's intersubjective storyworld, they can be only approximated for a given imagined community of authors and recipients. A manga's referential meaning remains thus deeply rooted within the social, whereas its individual picture objects are independent from cultural codes and communicative intentions, if the iconic threshold of surrogate stimuli is sufficiently exceeded.

3. Pictoriality and Representational Correspondence

An interesting question arises then: Where exactly do we draw the conceptual line between the picture object (in front of our eyes) and the storyworld object (supposed to exist "somewhere else")? How much of what we see "in" the picture object is part of its referential meaning? We could rephrase this problem as to whether the "style" of any graphic representation is in *representational correspondence* to the represented situation (Figure 1): "For a given representational work, only certain features of the representation serve to represent features of the things represented."[40] Let us address the intuition why we would usually *not* suppose that the style of graphic representations can be "mapped" from the picture object to the referential meaning. We expect a represented world "beyond" the single picture that is not black and white, for instance, and not pervaded by "visible outlines." Arguing from narratological theory, we could find support for this by something akin to Marie-Laure Ryan's *principle of minimal departure*, stating that "the imagination will consequently conceive fictional storyworlds on the model of the real world, and it will import knowledge from the real world to fill out incomplete descriptions."[41]

We thus hold certain assumptions with regard to the *kind of represented world*, and we "fill up the gaps" accordingly.[42] But this is a *judgment* on the "likeness" of the represented world to ours. Taken a step further, this judgment can be far more consequential if we apply it, for instance, to the appearances of *bodies* of the represented characters. While this is a problem not very central to Natsume, one of the most far-reaching claims in Itô Gô's groundbreaking *Tezuka Is Dead: Hirakareta manga hyôgenron he* (Toward an enlightened theory of manga expressions, 2005) is that we must precisely *not* think of represented manga-characters as having "regular bodies" made out of flesh and blood.[43] This is especially relevant with regard to the myriad "cartoon characters" that (on the level of picture objects) can be seen as anthropomorphic hybrids of animals, objects, or humans (compare this to Thomas Lamarre's account of the "plastic line" or the "cartoon line").[44] Itô argued, for instance, that the "frog" Beshi or the "caterpillar" Kemunpasu (both from Akatsuka Fujio's 1967 slapstick-manga *Môretsu Atarô*) are "decidedly nonhuman and not even representations of an actual frog and caterpillar, but their existence is certainly recognized as something with personality."[45] Such proto-characters *(kyara)*, mere "abstractions from the human body" whose "identity is malleable, gender merely a suggestion," are semiotically challenging.[46] If Itô and many others are right, we would need to postulate a special "plane" reserved to all those features we clearly see "in" the picture objects, but that (for whatever reason) cannot be taken as "valid" in terms of their referential meaning. Packard, stating one of the most consequential observations within contemporary comics theory, spoke of a "semiotic third space" or a "parasitic tertiary signification" in which the "duckness" of Donald Duck would rest *if* we were to decide that the Ducks were not represented ducks— but "actually" humans, represented *as* Ducks.[47] The semiotic third space is precisely the level of the picture object *if it is not* in representational correspondence to the level of referential meaning. Or the other way around: If we have reasons to believe that the assumed appearance of objects within some possible lifeworld it is not meant to be taken "literally" from what we see on the page, then it must be confined to the semiotic third space. This is clearly the case in Art Spiegelman's *Maus* in which Jewish people are represented *as mice*, which is clearly in no way "literal."

But the semiotic third space must be taken into account, I propose, in any and all pictorial representations in comics and manga, even (and maybe especially) in cases where the protagonists are clearly meant to be understood as being human. Think of the stylistic manga device of *chibi*: characters "turning" into emoticon versions of themselves during moments of emotional duress. Although the visible picture objects (that we see "in" the lines) can look radically different from each other, they are still "held together" by same invisible referential identity on the level of the storyworld. To quote Packard again: "[C]artoons show us human bodies without showing us what they look like."[48] I think it is useful, then, to consider picture objects first and foremost as three-dimensional projections out of two-dimensional inscriptions. As Göran Sonesson puts it: "The sole property of which the picture object cannot be deprived is its three-dimensionality."[49] Everything else (that is "added" to the referential meaning, or "subtracted" to the semiotic third space) must be inferred from our prior knowledge about or our general expectation of the given storyworld in question.

Prototypical pictures such as real-life films might be able to exploit the "closeness to perception" to such a degree that almost *everything* we see "in" a picture can be taken as valid for the storyworld. Only then, the semiotic third space seems to disappear or become completely transparent. Such a "mapping," however, is rarely complete, as I have argued elsewhere in more detail.[50] I find it helpful therefore to regard picture objects in comics as similar to a theater stage. The actors on a stage may represent fictional entities by using their bodies and some physical props, while pictures use surrogate stimuli. Both, however can never actually "show" fictional entities like characters, for the same reason that no audience member in a theater can save the represented heroine by jumping on stage: "One person can save another only if they live in the same world. *Cross-world* saving is ruled out, and for similar reasons so is cross-world killing, congratulating, handshaking and so forth."[51] The same holds true for cross-world perception.

4. Pictoriality and the Pictogrammatic Symbols of Manga

Having established that a clear distinction must be maintained between the picture objects (that we can see) and the referential meaning (that we can intersubjectively construct as part of the storyworld), I would like to go back to the fascinating question of whether *all* pictorial signs of manga must be connected to represented storyworld objects ("behind" their appearances). If not, what would be minimal criteria for that mysterious "emergence"? There are many ways to approach this complicated problem, and I cannot hope to give a definite answer here. Instead, I want to focus on Natsume again, indicating some of the possible answers that his observations on manga suggest. Looking closely on his examples, picture objects are not always represented as *existing* (and, therefore, as being *perceptible*) in any possible world at all. In comics and manga, there are in fact countless picture objects lacking any storyworld entities that they could be in any "correspondence." This becomes evident if we look at conventionalized pictogrammatic symbols, such as sweat beads or all of those little stars, birds, or steam clouds emanating from characters' heads. Those kinds of signs are widely recognized as important parts of comics' and manga's vocabulary, although under widely different terms such as "comicana," "bound morphemes," "pictorial runes," or simply "multimodal metaphors."[52] Natsume's and Takekuma's conception of *kei'yu* (literally "shape-metaphors" or "metaphoric forms") and *man'pu* ("manga-specific signs"), terms they proposed together in 1995 and refined again and again, attributes much more theoretical prominence to them.[53] But they also raise reasonable doubt as to whether these signs are in fact easily distinguishable from "regular" pictures of manga.

Initially, Natsume and Takekuma are not at all arguing against the commonsense notion that pictogrammatic manga symbols are conventionalized visual metaphors. Or, as McCloud put it before them: "Taken out of their original context, [visual metaphors] can now be applied anywhere . . . approaching the abstract status of linguistic symbols."[54] Natsume is similarly fascinated by the fact that such symbols "underwent a gradual abstraction process within manga, to become conventional signs."[55] To all these authors, the sweat bead is initially "based upon visual data."[56] By means of iconic conventions, a simple rounded shape is perceivable "as" a physical drop of liquid, if placed in the appropriate part of a facial representation. As a conventionalized symbol, however, it underwent a "drift from visible to invisible,"[57] or again with Natsume: "The sweat bead had initially a physical existence, but it underwent a psychological transformation."[58] In his attempt at a taxonomy of manga signs, however, the latter author adds two important aspects. First, he takes any "pictorial meaning" not as a starting point for subsequent metaphorization but as a different kind of *line-expressions* that can also assume "transformed" meanings (like affect lines, anger lines, and so on). Second, he identifies a fine-grained spectrum *in between* the poles of the visible and the invisible. Lines in manga can depict physical things, although in an exaggerated or perceptually abstracted way. They can also represent physical things that *could* be seen in principle but not in a static picture (like movement). Then, they can indicate physical things that can be perceived, although not by visual means, such as different smells (this, too, is McCloud's concern).[59] Finally, lines can become "symbols for psychological states not related to physical things at all."[60] Those are best understood as "autonomous modifiers."[61] Such *transformations of meaning* can be observed with regard to specific authors, genres, or styles, so that many kei'yu of prewar manga seem clearly out of date now. However, many of these conventions seem "defined like a noun."[62]

A picture of a light bulb, for instance, can be used as a kei'yu, if placed over a character's head. It then becomes a conventionalized way to represent that he or she experiences a sudden realization. In this specific case, we cannot speak of a *gradual* pictorial abstraction but rather have to acknowledge "manga-internal transformations of a sign into an interior, psychological metaphor."[63] From the perspective of picture theory, I would claim that this difference—representing a physical light bulb versus using the light bulb to represent that a character is experiencing a revelation—is tremendous. If we use it as a kei'yu, then the light bulb is quite simply representing *that* a character is experiencing a sudden realization, without determining in any way what this experience must feel (or "look") like. In other words (and this will hardly come as a surprise), kei'yu function exactly like pictograms. A pictogram is a graphic configuration that may be understood as a picture, but this picture is itself a (more or less) conventionalized symbol. Its pictoriality is relevant only insofar as it lets recipients infer the appropriate assertion (*that* something is the case within the diegesis). Takekuma speaks about the "necessity of manga pictures to have a high efficiency in transmitting meaning."[64] They are thus more propositional than phenomenal. The picture theoretical consequence is not only that their "closeness to perception" is drastically reduced. It also means that we have no *pictorial* gap between picture object and referential meaning, because there is no "perceptual plane" in the first place on which to "map" the surrogate stimuli.

In the case of the light bulb, it usually *must* be decided on which side of the "threshold" we are: either there is a physical thing within the storyworld or there is not. And, as with other kinds of visual puns before, the violation of this principle provides a stable source of humor in comics, manga, and animated films alike. But many instances of kei'yu are far more open to interpretation. Following Natsume, it is not at all clear whether a little dust cloud (next to a clash or an impact) is meant to be taken as a "manga-like exaggeration" of a physical and thus visible phenomenon (dust, stirred up by the impact)[65] or, rather, as a representation of an invisible phenomenon (an impact that *feels*, to a character, "like an explosion"). Takekuma argued that, if we see a character with a giant teardrop in the corner of his or her eye, it does not necessarily mean that there is a visible phenomenon of that size—merely that the character is crying, or maybe not even that: maybe it just represents that he or she *feels like crying*.[66] If this is taken seriously, then we would need to question whether any and all visible picture objects "actually" are allowed to be mapped on the diegetic level of referential meaning, or whether they are assigned to the semiotic third space. Natsume discusses many manga conventions by comparing them to the expressions of traditional Japanese theatre forms such as Kabuki:[67] a scene can, diegetically, take place in pitch black darkness, while it is clearly visible to the audience, and so on. This points again to the fact that what we *see* even on a theater stage is still just a representation, not the represented situation, character, or world itself (even if a stage representation is even closer to perception than a pictorial one).

In general, all that has been said should hold true for cinema and animated film as well. The only reason I see why the picture object/referential meaning gap has so rarely been paid attention to is that indexical (photochemically recorded) images have mostly been taken as the "unmarked case." This is unfortunate, I think, not least because it produces blind spots where photographic images, too, cannot be taken "verbatim," i.e., where they are not in representational correspondence. I am not just thinking of obvious examples, like Lars von Trier's *Dogville* (2003), where we clearly perceive a theater stage "in" the film that is meant to represent a "regular" town.[68] More subtle und troublesome questions regarding the conflation of actors' and characters' bodies (or rather their respective appearances) are in play in most or all live-action film, as Thon has argued.[69] In manga, however, we can never evade these questions. Following Packard, even the most realistically drawn backgrounds often do not represent physical spaces but rather abstract possibilities for the emergence of narrative events:

> A forest will appear with any number of trees of changing shape and placement, yet no contradiction will be observed by readers; a house will have an indeterminate number of windows, wall paintings, pieces of furniture, and indeed interior walls, as no attempt is made to piece together the building as a whole while characters move through the space they inhabit.[70]

So, what does all of this mean? Any picture in comics and manga can possess a quite "open signification" that must not be taken at face value.[71] This, finally, is where we should agree most with Ôtsuka's or Natsume's claims that "manga expressions are an accumulation of conventions."[72] The "closeness to perception" of comic and manga pictures relies thus on a very gradual evaluation, at least in terms of their referential meaning. If this is true, then we should not treat "pictoriality" in manga as a singular phenomenon (opposed to other, more verbal "modes"). Instead, I find it helpful to adopt Charles Hatfield's account of medium-specific *tensions* between modes of signification:

> In most comics, the symbols that show are representational drawings while the symbols that tell are words, balloons, and a few familiar icons. . . . But the potential exists for comics creators to push this tension much further, even to incorporate representational drawings as 'dialogue' and to blur the difference between alphabetic symbols and pictures. At its broadest level, then, what we call verbal/visual tension may be characterized as the clash and collaboration of *different codes of signification,* whether or not written words are used.[73]

In other words, comics' and manga's medium-specific tensions cannot be distributed on two sides of an alleged verbal/visual-divide.

5. Pictoriality Between Material and Affordance, Manga between the Individual and the Social

This article set out from the commonplace notion that manga are *multimodal* forms of expressions because they combine words and pictures. Since the mode of "pictoriality" is far from clearly defined, however, I took recourse to Natsume Fusanosuke's manga poetics, which conceptualize "pictures" as an inherently problematic category within a larger arrangement of material conditions and semiotic affordances. To speak of "pictures" in manga is only possible by virtue of one of many effects that the "fascination of the line" holds over recipients. I tried to show that, whatever one's preference for terminology, one should account for two distinct thresholds of pictorial meaning (Figure 1). Many of the humorous-gag manga Natsume discusses playfully subvert the "regular" conventions by which these thresholds are usually kept invisible—but they are present in every work. The first would be the threshold of iconic categorization according to certain cognitive faculties. If a *relevant amount of surrogate stimuli* is provided by graphical means, recipients are able to see three-dimensional configurations "in" surfaces of two-dimensional inscriptions: picture objects emerge. The second threshold concerns the assumption of individuated entities within diegetic planes— storyworlds or possible worlds—on which these stimuli can be more or less closely "mapped." This plane, which can only be "accessed" as an intersubjective approximation, can be called the picture object's referential meaning. While both thresholds have to be distinguished from each other, this distinction involves an evaluation of the respective "closeness to perception" of the picture object, that is, how relevant the perceptual information of the material is to our epistemic knowledge about the referential meaning (as "valid" parts of a given storyworld).

Only the former threshold can be seen to rely on perceptual competences and material conditions, while an assessment of the latter involves acquaintance with (and a judgment about) culturally, historically, and especially generically situated conventions. These will always be embedded in specific communicative situations: particular manga in specific publication formats. Although it has not been at the center of this article, these communicative situations must not be reduced to a kind of author-recipient relationship either. Instead, we must acknowledge the "existence of specific communities" in "collaborative networks,"[74] as well as the anticipation of "secondary productions" (fan-produced work).[75] Most communicative situations will thus be classified (or *framed*) by the recipients as belonging to a certain type of media, such as prototypical manga. Gunther Kress and Theo van Leeuwen call such classes of (multimodal) texts simply "genres,"[76] but that might not be so different from a specific "medium conventionally perceived as distinct":[77] a culturally defined *form of media*, such as manga. In order to account for the semiotic affordances of manga's material conditions, it is accordingly necessary to distinguish between the *modality* of pictoriality and the *mediality* of pictoriality.

Many important conclusions concerning manga's materiality can be drawn from these observations. The mediality of manga differs from very "similar" material conditions in other medial contexts. Within the medial frame of "a manga" we usually assume a storyworld "behind" or "beyond" the given representations—if we are to relate *not more than two* consecutive frames to each other by inferring some kind of spatiotemporal coherence between them (or, more precisely, between their picture objects). This is very different from what we presuppose in pictograms, emoji, or in many traffic sign (i.e., in pictorial signs in other communicative contexts), even though they might employ the same material affordances to generate similar picture objects. Admitting that the pictures of comics and manga, by their mediality—by their conventionalized utilization within a culturally framed, communicative system mediating between agents and actors—usually *do* represent individuated entities located within possible worlds, however, does not at all dictate how "close to perception" these representations are in terms of representational correspondence. It is not at all obvious that manga pictures "prescribe imaginations," to use Kendall Walton's terms again, to imagine their characters to be either "realistic" or very "abstract." There might thus be a larger or a smaller "gap" between the picture object that we actually see "in" the material lines, and what they might "actually" look like to an observer within their assumed diegetic domain. This is where the mediality of manga is not just embedded within the social; more to the point, an essential part of the mediality of manga is *comprised of* a conventional-institutional and thus social dimension. Following Jaqueline Berndt, this allows to speak of a manga as "media" in the first place, formed by the "conventionalized practices and institutional frameworks, which, once established, predetermine how individual mediums [material carriers] are being used."[78] The conceptual distinction between both levels of pictorial meaning— for which Natsume provided clearer descriptions than many other scholars in international literature—allows us to see how the materialities of line drawings offer affordances to manga artists not available in other media, precisely because their correspondence must never be taken as a given.

·····

Dr. Lukas R. A. Wilde is a post-doctoral research associate at Tübingen University's Department of Media Studies. He studied theater and media studies, Japanese studies, and philosophy at the Friedrich-Alexander-University Erlangen-Nürnberg and the Gakugei University of Tokyo, and was a fellow of the German National Scholarship Foundation. Wilde's dissertation investigated the communicative functions of "characters" *(kyara)* within contemporary Japanese society. His main areas of interest are visual communication, picture and media theory, webcomics and digital comics. In the German Society for Comic Studies (ComFor) Wilde is the executive board's treasurer, as well as one of the spokespersons of the Committee for Comic Studies (AG Comicforschung) of the German Society of Media Studies (GfM). Lukas Wilde was awarded the Roland-Faelske-Prize in 2018 for the best dissertation in Comics and Animation Studies. A list of publications can be found at http://lukasrawilde.de/en.

·····

Acknowledgments
I would like to thank Christopher Low, Julian Scherer, Anand Krishna, and Jan-Noël Thon for linguistic support, valuable observations, and a healthy amount of criticism. All translations from Japanese and German sources are my own.

Notes
1. James Elkins, *On Pictures and the Words That Fail Them* (Cambridge: Cambridge University Press, 1998), xi.
2. Ôtsuka Eiji, *Sengo manga no hyôgen kûkan: Kigôteki shintai no jubaku* (The expressive space of postwar Manga: The spell of semiotic bodies) (Kyoto: Hôsôkan, 1994), 10–11.
3. Natsume Fusanosuke and Takekuma Kentarô, eds., *Manga no yomikata* (How to read manga) (Tokyo: Takarajima-sha, 1995).
4. Scott McCloud, *Understanding Comics: The Invisible Art* (New York: Harper Perennial, 1993), 129; Natsume Fusanosuke, *Manga wa naze omoshiroi no ka: Sono hyôgen to bunpô* (What makes manga fascinating? On expressions and grammar) (Tokyo: NHK, 1997), 66.
5. Natsume, *Manga wa naze omoshiroi no ka,* 84.
6. Takekuma Kentarô, "*Koma ni okeru 'shutai' to 'kyakutai': Manga no koma wa nani kara dekite iru ka*" (The "subjects" and "objects" of panels: What are manga-panels composed of?), in Natsume and Takekuma, *Manga no yomikata,* 76–77.
7. Itô Gô, *Tezuka isu deddo: Hirakareta manga hyôgenron he* (Towards an enlightened theory of manga expressions) (Tokyo: NTT Shuppan, 2005), 122.

8. Natsume, *Manga wa naze omoshiroi no ka*, 66.
9. Caroline Levine, *Forms: Whole, Rhythm, Hierarchy, Network* (Princeton: Princeton University Press, 2015), 5.
10. Natsume, *Manga wa naze omoshiroi no ka*, 76.
11. Natsume, *Manga wa naze omoshiroi no ka*, 73.
12. Natsume, *Manga wa naze omoshiroi no ka*, 52.
13. Natsume, *Manga wa naze omoshiroi no ka*, 76.
14. Natsume, *Manga wa naze omoshiroi no ka*, 77.
15. Natsume, *Manga wa naze omoshiroi no ka*, 71.
16. Natsume, *Manga wa naze omoshiroi no ka*, 69.
17. Klaus Sachs-Hombach and Jörg R. J. Schirra, "To Show and to Say: Comparing the Uses of Pictures and Language," *Studies in Communication Science* 7, no. 2 (2007): 35–62; Klaus Sachs-Hombach, "Theories of Image: Five Tentative Theses," in *What Is an Image? The Stone Art Theory Institutes Vol. 2*, ed. James Elkins and Maja Naef, 229–32 (University Park: Pennsylvania State University Press, 2011).
18. Richard Wollheim, "On Pictorial Representation," *Journal of Aesthetics and Art Criticism* 56, no. 3 (1998): 217–26.
19. Lambert Wiesing, *Artifizielle Präsenz: Studien zur Philosophie des Bildes* (Artificial presence: Studies on the philosophy of pictures) (Frankfurt am Main: Suhrkamp, 2005), 37–80.
20. Wolfram Pichler and Ralph Ubl, *Bildtheorie: Zur Einführung* (Introduction to picture theory) (Hamburg: Junius, 2016), 27.
21. Umberto Eco, *Kant and the Platypus: Essays on Language and Cognition* (London: Vintage, 2000), 353–82.
22. Lukas R. A. Wilde, "The Elephant in the Room of Emoji-Research, or: Pictoriality, to what Extent?" in *Emoticons, Kaomoji, and Emoji: The Transformation of Communication in the Digital Age*, ed. Elena Giannoulis and Lukas R. A. Wilde (New York: Routledge, 2020).
23. Eco, *Kant and the Platypus*, 382–86.
24. Börries Blanke, *Vom Bild zum Sinn: Das ikonische Zeichen zwischen Semiotik und analytischer Philosophie* (From the pictorial to the meaningful: The iconic sign between semiotics and analytical philosophy) (Wiesbaden: Deutscher Universitätsverlag, 2003), 107–14.
25. Neil Cohn, *The Visual Language of Comics: Introduction to the Structure and Cognition of Sequential Images* (London: Bloomsbury, 2013), 23–33, 153–59.
26. Natsume, *Manga wa naze omoshiroi no ka*, 73.
27. Paul Wells, *Understanding Animation* (London: Routledge, 1998), 131–34.
28. Natsume, *Manga wa naze omoshiroi no ka*, 82.
29. Ibid., 91.
30. Marie-Laure Ryan, "Towards a Definition of Narrative," in *The Cambridge Companion to Narrative*, ed. David Herman, 22–38 (Cambridge: Cambridge University Press, 2007), 29.

31. Stephan Packard, *Anatomie des Comics: Psychosemiotische Medienanalyse* (Anatomy of comics: Psycho-semiotic media analysis) (Göttingen: Wallstein Verlag, 2006), 180.

32. Natsume, *Manga wa naze omoshiroi no ka*, 79.

33. Natsume, *Manga wa naze omoshiroi no ka*, 82.

34. Ole Frahm, "Weird Signs: Comics as Means of Parody," in *Comics & Culture: Analytical and Theoretical Approaches to Comics,* ed. Anne Magnussen and Hans-Christian Christiansen, 177–91 (Copenhagen: Museum Tusculanum University Press of Copenhagen, 2000); Steven Surdiacourt, "Image & Narrative #8: Tying Ends Together: Surface and Storyworld in Comics," http://comicsforum.org/2012/12/27/image-narrative-8-tying-ends-together-surface-and-storyworld-in-comics-by-steven-surdiacourt (accessed August 8, 2018).

35. Jan-Noël Thon, *Transmedial Narratology and Contemporary Media Culture* (Lincoln: University of Nebraska Press (2016), 53–56.

36. Uri Margolin, "Character," in *The Cambridge Companion to Narrative,* ed. David Herman, 66–79 (Cambridge: Cambridge University Press, 2007), 71.

37. Kendall L. Walton, *Mimesis as Make-Believe: On the Foundations of the Representational Arts* (Cambridge, Mass.: Harvard University Press, 1993), 35–43.

38. Thon, *Transmedial Narratology,* 353; original emphasis.

39. Wollheim, "On Pictorial Representation," 217.

40. Gregory Currie, *Narratives and Narrators: A Philosophy of Stories* (Oxford: Oxford University Press, 2010), 59.

41. Marie-Laure Ryan, "Story/Worlds/Media: Tuning the Instruments of a Media-Conscious Narratology," in *Storyworlds across Media: Toward a Media-Conscious Narratology,* ed. Marie-Laure Ryan and Jan-Noël Thon, 25–49 (Lincoln: University of Nebraska Press, 2014), 35.

42. Thon, *Transmedial Narratology,* 60.

43. Itô Gô, *Tezuka isu deddo,* 109–76; Itô Gô, "Manga History Viewed through Proto-Characteristics," in *Tezuka: The Marvel of Manga,* ed. Philip Brophy, 107–13 (Melbourne: National Gallery of Victoria, 2006).

44. Thomas Lamarre, "Manga Bomb: Between the Lines of Barefoot Gen," in *Comics Worlds and the World of Comics: Towards Scholarship on a Global Scale,* ed. Jaqueline Berndt, 262–307 (Kyoto: International Manga Research Center, Kyoto Seika University, 2010), 280–87.

45. Itô, "Manga History," 108.

46. Inoue Yasushi, "Manga gengo sekai ga umidashita (chô)kigô kyara ni tsuite: Itô Gô 'Tezuka izzu deddo' ni yosate" (On *kyara* and innovative (super)symbols in the world of manga linguistics: A critique of 'Tezuka Is Dead' by Itô Gô), *Journal of Kyôto Seika University* 京都精華大学 32 (2007): 162–85, 175; Lukas R. A. Wilde, "Kyara Revisited: The Pre-Narrative Character-State of Japanese Character Theory," Characters Across Media, special-themed issue of Frontiers of Narrative Studies 5, no. 2 (2019): 220–47.

47. Packard, *Anatomie des Comics*, 137; Stephan Packard, "The Drawn-Out Gaze of the Cartoon: A Psychosemiotic Look at Subjectivity in Comic Book Storytelling," in *Subjectivity across Media: Interdisciplinary and Transmedial Perspectives*, ed. Maike S. Reinerth and Jan-Noël Thon, 111–24 (New York: Routledge, 2017); Stephan Packard. "How Factual are Factual Comics? Parasitic Imaginations in Referential Cartoons," in *Comics Meets Science: Proceedings of the Symposium on Communicating and Designing the Future of Food in the Anthropocene*, ed. Reinhold Leinfelder, Alexandra Hamann, Jens Kirstein, and Marc Schleunitz, 19–27 (Berlin: Christian A. Bachmann, 2017).

48. Packard, "How Factual are Factual Comics?" 24.

49. Göran Sonesson, *Pictorial Concepts: Inquiries into the Semiotic Heritage and its Relevance to the Interpretation of the Visual World* (Lund: Lund University Press, 1989), 272.

50. Lukas R. A. Wilde, *Im Reich der Figuren: Meta-narrative Kommunikationsfiguren und die 'Mangaisierung' des japanischen Alltags* (Empire of characters: Meta-narrative communicational characters and the 'manga-ization' of everyday Japan) (Köln: Herbert von Halem, 2018), 173–213; "The Epistemology of the Drawn Line: Abstract Dimensions of Narrative Comics," in *Abstraction and Comics/La BD et l'abstraction*, Vol. II, ed. Aarnoud Rommens, Benoît Crucifix, Björn-Olav Dozo, Erwin Dejasse, and Pablo Turnes, 9–32 (Liege: La 5e Couche, 2019).

51. Walton, *Mimesis as Make-Believe*, 195; original emphasis.

52. Mort Walker, *Lexicon of Comicana* (Bloomington: iUniverse, 1980); Cohn, *The Visual Language of Comics*, 34; Charles Forceville, "Pictorial Runes in Tintin and the Picaros," *Journal of Pragmatics* 43 (2011): 875–90; Bart Eerden, "Anger in Asterix: The Metaphorical Representation of Anger in Comics and Animated Films," in *Multimodal Metaphor: Applications of Cognitive Linguistics*, ed. Charles Forceville, 243–64 (Berlin: de Gruyter, 2009); Kazuko Shinohara and Yoshihiro Matsunaka, "Pictorial Metaphors of Emotion in Japanese Comics," in *Multimodal Metaphor: Applications of Cognitive Linguistics*, ed. Charles Forceville, 265–96 (Berlin: de Gruyter, 2009).

53. Natsume, "Manga byôsen genron"; Natsume Fusanosuke, "'Ase' no hyôgen ni miru 'keiyu' no shinkaron" (A Theory of 'kei'yu' Development with respect to the 'Sweat Bead'-Expression), in Natsume and Takekuma, *Manga no yomikata*, 106–11; Natsume Fusanosuke, "Manga no shinkocchô 'kei'yu' to ha nani ka: Manga-teki kigô no bunrui no kokoromi" (What are manga's 'kei'yu' really made of? An attempt at a taxonomy of mangaesque signs), in Natsume and Takekuma, *Manga no yomikata*, 112–15; Takekuma, "Koma ni okeru 'shutai' to 'kyakutai'"; Natsume, *Manga wa naze omoshiroi no ka*, 84–89.

54. McCloud, *Understanding Comics*, 129.

55. Natsume, *Manga wa naze omoshiroi no ka*, 86.

56. McCloud, *Understanding Comics*, 130.

57. McCloud, *Understanding Comics*, 130.

58. Natsume, "Manga no shinkocchô 'kei'yu' to ha nani ka," 112.

59. McCloud, *Understanding Comics*, 128.

60. Natsume, "Manga no shinkocchô 'kei'yu' to ha nani ka," 112.

61. Natsume *Manga wa naze omoshiroi no ka*, 84.

62. Natsume "Manga no shinkocchô 'kei'yu' to ha nani ka," 115.

63. Natsume "Manga no shinkocchô 'kei'yu' to ha nani ka," 113.

64. Takekuma, "Koma ni okeru 'shutai' to 'kyakutai,'" 78.

65. Natsume, "Manga no shinkocchô 'kei'yu' to ha nani ka," 112.

66. Takekuma, "Koma ni okeru 'shutai' to 'kyakutai,'" 78.

67. Natsume, *Manga wa naze omoshiroi no ka*, 89.

68. *Dogville*, dir. Lars von Trier (Lions Gate, 2003).

69. Jan-Noël Thon, "Transmedial Narratology Revisited: On the Intersubjective Construction of Storyworlds and the Problem of Representational Correspondence in Films, Comics, and Video Games," *Narrative* 25, no. 3 (2017): 286–320.

70. Stephan Packard, "Closing the Open Signification: Forms of Transmedial Storyworlds and Chronotopoi in Comics," *Transmedial Worlds in Convergent Media Culture*, special-themed issue of *StoryWorlds: A Journal of Narrative Studies* 7, no. 2 (2015): 55–74, 69.

71. Packard, "Closing the Open Signification," 69.

72. Natsume, *Manga wa naze omoshiroi no ka*, 83.

73. Hatfield, Charles, "An Art of Tension," in *A Comics Studies Reader*, ed. Jeet Heer and Kent Worcester, 132–48 (Jackson: University Press of Mississippi, 2009), 134; original emphasis.

74. Jaqueline Berndt, "Ghostly: 'Asian Graphic Narratives,' Nonnanba, and Manga," in *From Comic Strips to Graphic Novels: Contributions to the Theory and History of Graphic Narrative*, ed. Daniel Stein and Jan-Noël Thon, 363–84 (Berlin: de Gruyter, 2013), 365; Ian Condry, *The Soul of Anime: Collaborative Creativity and Japan's Media Success Story* (Durham: Duke University Press, 2013), 15–53.

75. Nele Noppe, *The Cultural Economy of Fanwork in Japan: Dôjinshi Exchange as a Hybrid Economy of Open Source and Cultural Goods* (Leuven: University of Leuven, Faculty of Arts, 2014).

76. Theo van Leeuwen, *Introducing Social Semiotics* (London: Routledge, 2005), 122–38; Gunther R. Kress, *Multimodality: A Social Semiotic Approach to Contemporary Communication* (London: Routledge, 2010). 107–20.

77. Irina O. Rajewsky, "Border Talks: The Problematic Status of Media Borders in the Current Debate about Intermediality," in *Media Borders, Multimodality and Intermediality*, ed. Lars Ellestöm, 51–68 (Basingstoke: Palgrave Macmillan, 2010), 61.

78. Jaqueline Berndt, "Introduction: Shôjo Mediations," in *Shôjo Across Media: Exploring 'Girl' Practices in Contemporary Japan*, ed. Jaqueline Berndt, Kazumi Nagaike, and Fusami Ogi, 1–21 (Basingstoke: Palgrave Macmillan, 2019), 7.

Conjoined by Hand

Aesthetic Materiality in Kouno Fumiyo's Manga
In This Corner of the World

JAQUELINE BERNDT

In recent years, content-driven, or representational, readings of anime and manga have been increasingly countered by mediatic approaches, but the main focus has been mainly on the materiality of platforms and institutions rather than that of signifiers and artifacts that afford certain mediations in the first place. Kouno Fumiyo's *In This Corner of the World (Kono sekai no kata-sumi ni)* provides an excellent case to explore manga's aesthetic materiality, last but not least because of its congenial adaptation to the animated movie of the same name directed by Katabuchi Sunao (Studio MAPPA, 2016).[1] This movie attests to what John Guillory has pointed out in a different context, namely, that "[r]emediation makes the medium as such visible."[2] Consequently, it is used below as a foil to highlight how Kouno's manga conjoins different materialities in a medium-specific way resting on the drawn line, print on paper, and the serial format of the narrative.

This article pursues manga mediality from the angle of materiality to approach forms as aesthetic affordances without reiterating a decontextualized formalism modeled on modernist notions of authorship and autonomous art. First, I will try to summarize the story as unimpaired as possible by considerations of medium specificity in order to demonstrate subsequently what attention to aesthetic materiality may lead the reader to see or rather to become: namely, a mature participant. Second, I focus on the precedence of hand-drawing as well as the variety of drawn lines, pointing out that in Kouno's case aesthetic materiality does not facilitate authorship (evinced by traces of the artist's hand) or the manga medium as an art form (evinced by modernist self-reflexivity as an attribute of the text itself), but commonality, a distributive agency that involves artist, characters, and readers bridging past and present. Then, I turn to what is more often associated with materiality, namely, the physicality of the publication medium. Instead of paper quality (i.e., the coarse and yellowish printing paper of Japanese editions so difficult to reproduce abroad), I foreground linework, lettering, and paneling as well as the physical placement of the individual installments within the magazine. I interpret these aspects as nonverbal statements about genre conventions and also correlate them with the theme of marginality touched upon already in the work's title. As a whole, I hope to demonstrate that the focus on manga materiality in the broad sense (that is, including a non-representationalist attention to forms of representation, mediation, distribution, and perception) allows for critical readings of popular fiction that acknowledge its inclusive potential.

In the course of the discussion, I refer time and again to aspects that distinguish *In This Corner of the World* from conventional manga as represented by the global bestsellers. Characteristic of Kouno's work is a conjoining of not only actors and times but also dispositions: it keeps with mangaesque conventions and twists them concurrently, occupying a third space between major franchise-prone productions and highly authorial expressions. While such a disposition applies to a significant number of Japanese graphic narratives—stretching from Tezuka Osamu and Ikeda Riyoko to Taniguchi Jirô, Asano Inio, and Kyô Machiko—it still easily escapes European or North American comics studies insofar as they are inclined to neatly sort between "graphic novels" as serious personal and political narratives on the one hand, and "comics and manga" as industrial, coded, and serial B-literature on the other hand.[3] Against this backdrop it raises wrong expectations to call manga like Kouno's "alternative," even if they appear slightly deviant within the mediascape that is locally and globally associated with Japan.

A Hand's Tale

Kouno's graphic narrative was serialized in the biweekly magazine *Manga Action* from January 2007 to January 2009. Whereas the Japanese book edition falls into three volumes, the translated English edition crams the whole 430 pages into one unwieldy volume to accommodate a type of consumption that rests less on serialization than in Japan.[4] In line with the structure of the original magazine series, the book edition begins with 3 unnumbered prologue chapters, which are followed by a total of 44 numbered chapters and one "Final Chapter," each forming a more or less self-contained short episode of mostly 8 (sometimes 12, 14, or 16) pages and ending with a punchline.

In This Corner of the World is the story of Suzu, a humble young woman who grows up in the Hiroshima delta, approximately 3 km away from the later epicenter of the atomic bomb. The actual plot begins in February 1944, when the nineteen-year-old is married off to the neighboring town of Kure. There she cooks, scrubs, and cares for her sick mother-in-law while the men are at work—her husband, Shûsaku, as a minor clerk at the navy's court-martial and her father-in-law as an engineer at the shipyard of what was then the largest naval base of the Japanese Empire. Foreign in this corner of the world and constantly scolded by her sister-in-law Keiko, Suzu has but one refuge: drawing. Already as a little girl, she compensated for her older brother's bossiness by depicting him as an ogre in short comic strips. In her new setting, drawing helps her to cope with the unfamiliar environment while keeping the repercussions of war at bay. In June 1945, Suzu loses both her niece Harumi and her right hand to a delayed-action bomb. Months later she learns of the death of her parents and the radiation sickness of her younger sister in Hiroshima, from where Suzu and Shûsaku take an orphan home in the end.

The manga's title refers to a collection of nonfictional texts, first published on the occasion of the twentieth anniversary of the Hiroshima bomb. But whereas that volume accentuated the place (*kono . . . katasumi de*: "in this corner") and Hiroshima at that,[5] Kouno uses a particle that may also indicate a direction (*kono . . . katasumi ni*: "into this corner"), connoting both the protagonist's move to another town and the reader's orientation to the wartime past. The animated movie of 2016, which drew broad public attention to Kouno's narrative, fueled primarily two readings of it: on the one hand as a war story, on the other as "a period drama about female forbearance"[6] (both more or less underpinned by the postwar discourse of Japanese self-victimization through feminization).[7] Whereas film critics found the war responsibility inadequately addressed,[8] the manga artist herself said that she wanted to show Hiroshima from a perspective other than the one naturalized in Japan: "Somehow I felt reluctant to watching and depicting things related to the atomic bomb. I think I don't like the fact that the 'atomic bomb' is immediately linked to 'peace.' As if it had bestowed peace on us!"[9]

Yet, the war is not the only driving narrative force, neither in the manga nor the animated movie. Although the movie gives the male characters more space and extends the social spectrum through their jobs, the women are at the center, Suzu and, as her counterpart, Keiko, who had been a modern girl and married out of love, but once widowed is to hand over her son to the in-laws and on top of that, to see her house in Kure's downtown demolished for firebreaks. The third historical type of woman is the courtesan Rin, whom Suzu encounters when she loses her way in the city, and who perishes in the bombardment of July 1945 together with the red-light district of Kure. The animated movie of 2016 marginalized Rin and concealed Shûsaku's premarital relationship with her, which facilitated its promotion as a story of growing marital love outside of Japan.

In view of the manga's remediation by the animated movie, *In This Corner of the World* appears to tell not only of war and love, but also of a drawing hand. Hosoma Hiromichi, who published a collection of meticulous observations on both works, maintains that the animated movie shifted the narrative's perspective completely from Suzu to her right hand.[10] Kouno herself acknowledged that shift for the third volume of the Japanese edition, stating in an interview, "that from this point on, it is the story of the hand."[11] As if heading for this shift from the outset, occasional panels feature a single hand placed against empty ground. This starts with the third prologue episode: In the last small panel on the bottom left (according to the Japanese reading direction just before turning the page), a hand holding a pencil stub ap-

Figure 1. Right: the last page of "Chapter 32 (June, year 18), left: the first page of "Chapter 33 (June, year 18 [1945])." Kouno Fumiyo, *Kono sekai no katasumi ni, ge* (*In This Corner of the World*, III) (Tokyo: Futabasha, 2009), 36–37. © Fumiyo Kouno, Futabasha 2009.

pears; eighteen pages—and, for Suzu, five years—later this panel reappears, except that now chopsticks point to the left propelling the reader forward. After the explosion of the delay-action bomb on the last page of chapter 32 (Figure 1), when it becomes clear that Suzu has lost not only her niece but also her drawing hand, the hand begins to lead a life of its own, first as a mental image: A panel with the bandaged arm stump is followed by one with the complete hand which sketches a shamrock that grows into a garden of paradise, with Harumi playing in it (Figure 2). In chapter 39, the hand descends from above and strokes consolingly Suzu's head as she kneels in her vegetable patch crying on August 15, 1945, after the Emperor's radio speech. And at the very end of the manga the hand even gains its own voice. Holding a pen, it opens the last chapter, and after having spoken to Suzu in the form of a letter composed of panels and handwritten monologue, it becomes visible again, sequentially placed in free space and now holding a brush with which it watercolors the remaining pages.

Figure 2. The return of the lost hand. Kouno Fumiyo, *Kono sekai no katasumi ni, ge* (*In This Corner of the World*, III) (Tokyo: Futabasha, 2009), 42–43. © Fumiyo Kouno, Futabasha 2009.

Haptic Participation

But in Kouno's manga the hand is far more than a motif that attracts attention to what it represents. Before any symbolism, it serves a pragmatic function, namely, to invite the reader into the storyworld. Whereas conventional manga employ close-ups of character faces, here close-ups of the hand assume that role. This already appears in the third prologue episode when Suzu is given a pencil by her classmate Mizuhara to do a drawing in his stead. While the right half of the double-page spread relates the situation in seven ruler-rimmed panels, the left half features two hand-drawn and almost empty rectangles that are slightly shaded on the lower left (Figure 3).

The upper one contains a tail-less speech balloon with Suzu's words; the lower one shows her hand drawing a brush stroke to the right, flanked by two more bubbles. Suzu's forearm, however, is part of the frame, which at this

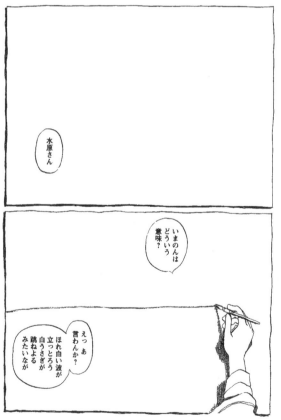

Figure 3. Suzu drawing. Kouno Fumiyo, *Kono sekai no katasumi ni, jô* (*In This Corner of the World*, I) (Tokyo: Futabasha, 2008a), 45. © Fumiyo Kouno, Futabasha 2008.

point bulges into the panel. As distinct from the animated movie, the comics medium is capable of making Suzu's hand the entry point to an empty space, which is at once the protagonist's drawing paper and the manga page in the reader's hand. The ensuing sensation of overlap is heightened on the following double-page spread, where the paper is drawn as if rising at the edges. Thus, the reader conjoins the protagonist in a concurrently representational and material way.

Discussing the specificity of comics as a paper-based medium and its persistence in the digital age, Katalin Orbán has highlighted how much comics rest on "print text [being] experienced as permanently integrated with its material base."[12] In reference to Alois Riegl, Orbán observes that "the sense of materiality is thus established mostly through a tactile relationship, in which hand-book contact and haptic visuality mutually inform each other."[13] While Laura U. Marks exemplified haptic vision with regard to video imagery and its grain,[14] in manga—a type of comics defined primarily as "line picture" (senga)[15]—haptic vision as an embodied form of seeing rests mainly on the drawn line. Drawing is one means of approximation, as anthropologist Michael Taussig observes: "A line drawn is not important for what it records as much as what it leads you to see."[16] This is inspired by John Berger's account of drawing, who actually went further than seeing: "Each confirmation or denial brings you closer to the object, until finally you are, as it were, inside it: the contours you have drawn no longer marking the edge of what you have seen, but the edge of what you have become."[17] Berger understands drawing primarily as an autobiographical record and applies it to the becoming of the artist, whereas in Kouno's manga the personal act of drawing goes beyond individualism; it serves commonality—between the characters as well as between artist, characters, and the readers who are being taken by hand and invited to eliminate historical distance, not simply looking at the past, but literally touching it.[18]

Kouno had previously experimented with such closeness in the six-page colored short story "Furui onna" (An old-fashioned woman, 2006).[19] Again, the protagonist is a young woman who appears to submit silently to Japan's modern patriarchy, and again she is an amateur artist, except that this time she draws on the bare back of leaflets. Emulating such a support, the pages on which the manga panels are laid out are imprinted with faint mirrored patterns, which seem to shine through from the leaflet's front. While this does not necessarily catch the eye upon first reading, on closer inspection it may ironically undercut the verbal affirmation of patriarchy and nationalism.

Here as elsewhere, Kouno calls upon her audience to maturely engage, at the risk of remaining politically vague herself.

In contrast to the water-colored *"Furui onna,"* the monochrome manga *In This Corner of the World* leans exclusively on graphism for layering different worlds, such as when it takes only one drawn line to conjoin the Bay of Kure and its battleships with their image in Suzu's sketch book (in chapter 12). The animated movie retains the discontinuous outlines of characters' faces and the little strokes on cheeks and arms, but it juxtaposes the different levels of perception primarily through distinction between graphic, or linework-based, and painterly renderings. Occasionally new sequences had to be created, for example, in the case of the colored target-marking bombs. While the manga relates their threat in one densely packed "hyperframe" panel in chapter 26, the animated movie first shows spots of color on a blue background, accompanied by sounds of detonation, before a hand with a brush enters the screen to set just such paint splotches onto the sky, thereby deferring the actual danger to another, aesthetic dimension, which can be read as escapism.

In the manga, the hand also presents itself as the subject materially, that is, through the very type of drawing. A particularly striking example appears in the middle of chapter 35, sixteen pages after the explosion of the delayed-action bomb. Here, Suzu monologizes in view of the ruined city of Kure, that it appears to her "as a world drawn with my left hand,"[20] which Kouno actually follows through with in her drawing of the images: "Halfway I decided to draw the background consistently with my left hand. Normally you would not get pages of such poor quality printed."[21] This especially stands out, as Kouno keeps to hand-drawn hatching, eschewing the use of screen tone. Due to her left-handed rendering the bars and struts of the room where Suzu sits in her sickbed futon (in chapter 35), consist of shaky lines, which the background artist of the animated movie, Hayashi Kôsuke, turned into broad impasto strokes, also brushed with the left.[22]

Drawn by Hand

In recent years, comics studies have advanced a more differentiated view on the collaboration between text and image, exploring variety within each of the two tracks.[23] The visual track of Kouno's manga is exceptionally rich in image formats. Some chapters contain diagrammatic representations of railway lines and timetables; others switch between panels that show Suzu sewing or cooking, and panels that serve as pictorial instructions for those activities, reminiscent of infographics. What the women learn in the air defense lessons is related through Suzu's notebook on the top half of six consecutive pages in chapter 29, and how the neighborhood association works is introduced in chapter 4 through the lyrics of a war-time song, the lines of which are accompanied by uniform picture boxes. In chapter 20, the panels even mimic dress patches with their dashed edges, alluding to Suzu's haphazard way of mending. But all these formats have in common that they are executed as freehand drawing. Not even urban spaces and their buildings assume a sharp-edged photorealistic look. Printed signs, posters and calendars are re-mediated by hand as are the extradiegetic historical explanations, placed as vertical Japanese script in the inner page margin (Figure 1). In addition to the laborious manual work that determined women's everyday life during the war, Kouno's freehand drawing associates both the "original contexts" of the re-presented mediums and their appropriation by Suzu or, more precisely, her hand.

But as dominant as free-handed drawing may be, the materiality of the drawn line itself changes with the tools. After the first prologue chapter, Kouno swaps the manga pen nib for a brush, evoking with water-saturated black ink the humidity of a summer's day in the tidal mudflats of Hiroshima Bay. The memories of Rin are rendered with a rouge brush, the utensil of the courtesan, which Suzu received from her with the advice: "Go on and make yourself pretty. / You know what they say . . . / When they clean up the bodies after a bombing, they start with the prettiest ones."[24] The most common alternation, however, is that between pen and pencil. While the pen stroke marks the diegetic present, the paler pencil outlines the domain of Suzu's imagination. It also sets itself apart from her everyday life in Kure materially: as pencil drawings are difficult to reproduce in printed manga, they were first copied and then glued into the artwork. A pencil is used for the short comic strips that caricature the older brother (five individual pages in total) as well as for the recurring heron, that associates with Suzu's past and hometown.[25] At the beginning, pencil drawings are located in thought bubbles—for example, when little Suzu pictures the candy she could buy—but mostly they serve two purposes: informative inserts (postcards or the neighborhood circular, for example) and panel frames that enclose retrospectives or mental images. The most representative example of the latter is the sequence in chapter 33 right after the explosion of the delayed-action bomb.

A large black panel opens that chapter, and then small panels with a freehand-drawn border appear, at first only occasionally interrupted by panels with the bold, ruler-rimmed standard frame (Figure 1). Gradually, it becomes clear that the penciled panels relate shreds of memory, which flicker through Suzu's feverish dreams: sewing sessions with the grandmother, the encounter with Rin, time spent with little Harumi. The bold panel frames—and with them the external reality—are gradually gaining the upper hand until the word "murderer" slips out of Keiko's mouth. The following page features the two already mentioned vignettes of Suzu's hand: first, the strongly contoured bandaged stump; second, the faintly outlined healthy hand (Figure 2).

This differentiation by line type is highly medium-specific (although not necessarily salient). Consequently, the animated movie expanded the big black panel at the beginning of chapter 33 to a whole sequence which, according to a handwritten note of the director in the storyboard, departs from cel animation in favor of "something like cine-calligraphy,"[26] i.e., the technique of direct engraving on filmstrips as developed by Norman McLaren with *Blinkity Blink* (1955). Accompanied by crackling noises, white lines flash. The voice of the grandmother can be heard and Suzu's monologue. Then the ground changes from black to white. The cel-animated colored figure of Suzu runs down a coastal path, indicated in gray lines, until a look at the bay, drawn with crayons, opens and Harumi can be seen and heard. Sound compensates for what stayed invisible in the manga's gutter.

Magazine Matters

Kouno conceived *In This Corner of the World* not as a book, but as a serial narrative, and published it in a magazine that appears to primarily target male readers judging from its cover photos and manga contents *(seinen manga)*.[27] In the Japanese context, this raises the issue of gendered genre. Does the cute-looking protagonist cater to a generically masculine gaze? Are elements of generically feminine manga fed into a masculine domain? The very fact that all kinds of visual formats are appropriated by the artist's, and through her Suzu's, hand may suggest an inclination to reducing otherness in a shôjo-mangaesque way.[28] Yet, significant formal characteristics of shôjo manga are missing: The linework is mainly rendered with a G-pen, a device that has shaped the appearance of graphic narratives for young men *(gekiga, seinen manga)*. In addition, screen tone is eluded as is the preference for printed script and more than two saliently alternating typefaces.

In contemporary manga, printed script predominates, for better readability as well as aesthetic transparency (that is, an access to characters and storyworld unimpeded by material concerns). Hand-lettering is by convention used for onomatopoeia and, in female genre tradition, extradiegetic, often funny comments on characters and situations.[29] Kouno, however, avoids such commitment to genre. Her manga leans on pictoriality rather than scripted text to evoke closeness, such as in the case of the drawing paper or the left-handedly drawn background. Her speech balloons are almost uniformly filled with printed characters. Handwritten onomatopoeiae are employed sparingly, until the manga's last third: when the sirens no longer seem to stop, the panels become superimposed by sound words that assume a ropelike physicality.

Furthermore, the paneling does not necessarily suggest affiliation with the genre of shôjo manga, which tends to foreground space, shifting the reader's attention back and forth between panel and page. And even if the G-pen plays a crucial role, an affiliation with seinen manga—which foregrounds the flow of time through transition from panel to panel—is not suggested either, although Kouno apparently invites the reader to proceed from panel to panel and from tier to tier, slightly offsetting the vertical gutters. Only in parallel montages of concurrent action is the grid geometrically accurate. This becomes evident, for example, on one page towards the end of chapter 32: Suzu and Harumi are sitting in an air raid bunker. To distract her niece, Suzu draws the faces of the family members into the dusty ground. While a sequence of vertically arranged sound words visualizes both the force and the length of the bombing, the underlying panel grid suggests less a process than a stagnation of time: The gaze of the characters, and the reader, while guided from right to left, is urged by onomatopoeiae to turn downward, which enforces the oppressiveness of the situation.

Such attention to the still space of the printed page manifests further in the occasional material juxtaposition of image and script. When Suzu lies on the sickbed and cannot yet make out reality, a horizontal panel suddenly appears in the middle tier across the entire double-page spread (chapter 33). It repeats an originally vertical panel showing Suzu and Shûsaku on a bridge and their reflection in the water (in chapter 15), which is now turned 45 degrees to the right. Compared to the panels on the upper and bottom tiers, the visible world appears reversed. The voices, however, remain in the medial "normality" as the speech balloons feature the Japanese dialogue in the usual vertical arrangement. Such a juxtaposition of seeing and reading direction can already be found in Kouno's first Hiroshima manga, the twenty-nine-page story "Town of Evening Calm" (*Yûnagi no machi*, 2003).[30] The protagonist, a young woman who feels guilty about having survived, suddenly runs up a vertical panel, away from the dead in the ground. But the Japanese lines of her monologue, which are to be read from top to bottom, pull back the reader's gaze after each upward movement, thus anticipating her eventual fall over (Figure 4).

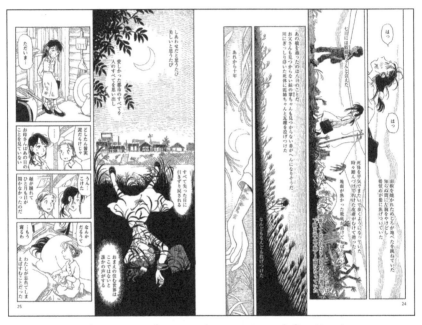

Figure 4. Material opposition of image and script in Kouno's first Hiroshima manga *Town of Evening Calm,* in Kouno Fumiyo, *Yûnagi no machi, sakura no kuni* (Tokyo: Futaba-sha, 2004), 24–25. © Fumiyo Kouno, Futabasha, 2004.

Considering the above, Kouno's graphic narrative clearly defies conventional genre attributions, and it even uses the physicality of the manga magazine to set itself apart from the genre of that very magazine, in this case, seinen manga: The installments of the series were placed between the table of contents, actually occupying the last page, and the back endpaper (Figures 5 and 6).

While popular series appear far ahead in a manga magazine, *In This Corner of the World* slipped into the last corner, like a humorous extra, a "gag manga," not to be taken too seriously.[31] The deliberately marginal positioning within the magazine began with chapter 2, when Suzu moved to Kure, a marginal "corner" of world history from the point of view of the atomic bombings. Seen from Kure, the atomic cloud of Hiroshima did not look like a mushroom, according to the image on the last page of chapter 37. But while this image suggests a peripheral, regionally specific view, manga critic Yoshimura Kazuma nationalizes it as Japanese in juxtaposion to the mushroom cloud as an icon established by American photographs.[32]

The material marginality of Suzu's experience is lost in remediation when two pages, which were initially published with an intermission of two weeks, come to form a double-page spread in the book edition. Likewise lost, especially in translated editions, is the intricate interplay of the format of serialization with the diegetic time of action: The frontispiece of chapter 1 indicates "December 18," which corresponds to the year Shôwa 18 (1943), but also Heisei 18 (2007), the release date of this manga chapter. In the apparently conservative reference to the imperial calendar, according to which, for example, the downfall of the Empire in 1945 does not necessarily appear to be a

Figure 5. Last page of chapter 32 upon first publication in magazine *Manga Action*, no. 13, 2008 (Futabasha). Bottom right margin: invitation to read also the next issue; left page: advertisement of a dating site, addressed to male readers. © Fumiyo Kouno, Futabasha 2008.

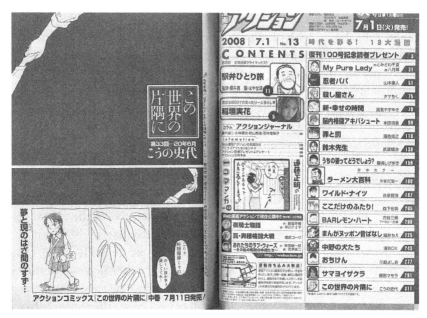

Figure 6. First page of chapter 33 upon first publication in magazine *Manga Action,* no. 14, 2008 (Futabasha). Right page: Table of Contents, with Kouno's title on the bottom right (indicating page 311). Bottom left: Editor's announcement that vol. 2 of the series will go on sale on July 11; left margin: "Suzu caught been between and reality." © Fumiyo Kouno, Futabasha 2008.

caesura (as the Shôwa era lasted from 1926 to 1989), the manga conjoins past and present yet again. Finally, it deserves mention how the dust jacket of the third Japanese volume anticipates unobtrusively the narrative's tragic climax by showing Suzu lying on her back with her arms straight up, but her right hand folded inward (Figures 7 and 8). This is easily overlooked, for example, in gallery exhibitions that give preference to framed color illustrations over monochrome paneled pages.

Conclusion

In This Corner of the World is an exercise in conjoining: the wartime past and the (in contemporary Japan) increasingly oblivious present, a politically charged history and the easily relatable personal act of drawing, haptic participation and critical contemplation. It accomplishes such conjoining through the deliberate employment of manga-specific materiality as grounded in the

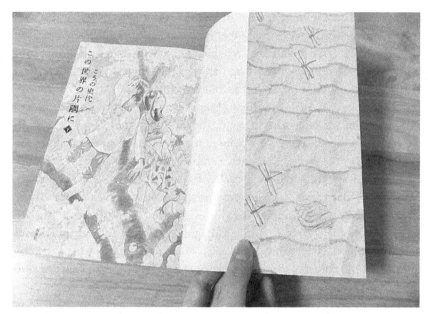

Figure 7. Dust jacket of vol. 3 of the Japanese edition (Kouno, 2009), in the reader's hand.

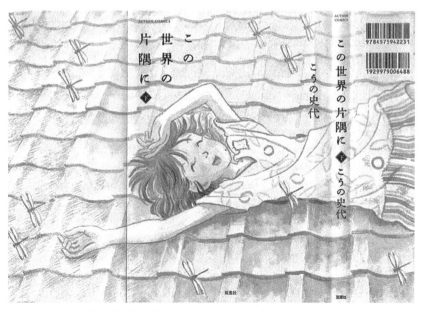

Figure 8. Dust jacket of vol. 3 of the Japanese edition (Kouno, 2009), unfolded. © Fumiyo Kouno, Futabasha 2009.

Japanese mediascape, so that parts of it may get lost in translation. With respect to the printed page as a site that conjoins multiple panels and as such different views, critic Nakamura Tadashi has highlighted the interplay of subjectivity and objectivity (or the imaginary and the symbolic) as characteristic of the manga medium in general and Kouno's manga in particular. Neither privileging one of the poles nor fusing them beyond recognition, *In This Corner of the World* indeed keeps a balance, juxtaposing different types of line within the same page space, redrawing printed matter by hand, and detaching the hand from Suzu in terms of character ontology. Ultimately, Suzu is anything but able to escape the harsh social reality qua imagination. Manga as a highly affective popular media has been promoting a relation between subjectivity and objectivity that resembles *sekai-kei*—"characterized by the immediate link between micro-condition, the protagonist's family and school (I), and macro-condition, concerning global crisis and ruin (world)."[33] In contradistinction, *In This Corner of the World* provides plentiful historical knowledge to the receptive, and margin-sensitive, reader.

But as indicated in this article's introduction, manga's medium specificity includes aesthetic form as much as sociocultural disposition. With regard to freehand drawing, the use of the pencil, and an emphasis on the sense of touch, the indifference towards genre, and furthermore its historical realism but lack of semantic straightforwardness, *In This Corner of the World* clearly deviates from what sells as "manga proper" in the domestic and global marketplace. At the same time, this graphic narrative cannot be denied distinctive manga features, ranging from magazine serialization and the centrality of a cute-looking character to the prioritization of closeness and affective participation over critical distance. Rather than presenting another, only this time Japanese, variant of "middlebrow" fiction located in between the modern dichotomy of high art and literature (or the "aesthetic disposition"), and industrial mass culture (or the "popular disposition"), Kouno's conjoining coincides with the "imagination-oriented disposition" of recent fan cultures that entwine the specialized expertise of the first with the penchant for sharing of the latter.[34] A focus on forms in their materiality rather than representation may help to illuminate such "third" disposition across fields.

....

Jaqueline Berndt is Professor in Japanese Language and Culture at Stockholm University. From 1991–2016, she taught in Japan, eventually at the Graduate School of Manga, Kyoto Seika University. Holding a first degree in Japanese

Studies (1987) and a PhD in Aesthetics/Art Theory from Humboldt University Berlin (1991), Berndt's academic work has been informed by media aesthetics and exhibition studies, and focused on graphic narratives, anime, and modern Japanese art. She has widely published in Japanese, German, and English; for example, the co-edited volume *Manga's Cultural Crossroads* (2013), and the monographs *Phänomen Manga* (1995) and *Manga: Medium, Art and Material* (2015). For more information see https://jberndt.net.

....

Notes

This article was first drafted as a keynote lecture for the joint annual conference of the working groups on animation and comics research within the German Association of Media Studies (GfM), in Hannover, November 2016; it is a revised version of Jaqueline Berndt, "Hand in Hand: Kouno Fumiyo's Mangaserie *Kono sekai no katasumi ni* (In this corner of the world) im Vergleich zur Anime-Adaptation durch Katabuchi Sunao," in *Ästhetik des Gemachten: Interdisziplinäre Beiträge zur Animations- und Comicforschung (The Aesthetics of Craftedness: Interdisciplinary Contributions to Animation and Comics Research)*, ed. Hans-Joachim Backe, Julia Eckel, Erwin Feyersinger, Véronique Sina and Jan-Noël Thon (Berlin: deGruyter, 2018). Open access edition: https://www.degruyter.com/view/product/485366?format=EBOK (accessed October 18, 2018).

1. The live-action film (Nihon TV *shûsen dorama supesharu* broadcast on August 5, 2011) did not make a significant public impact. Following the unexpected popularity of the animated movie of 2016, TBS produced and broadcasted a TV mini-series (July–September 2018, 9 × 54 min.). A prolonged version of the animated movie was released in December 2019 *(Kono sekai no (sarani ikutsumono) katasumi ni)*.
2. John Guillory, "Genesis of the Media Concept," *Critical Inquiry* 36, no. 2 (Winter 2010): 324.
3. Jan Baetens, Hugo Frey, and Stephen E. Tabachnick, "Introduction," in *The Cambridge History of the Graphic Novel* (Cambridge: Cambridge University Press; Kindle Edition), 10-11.
4. Kouno Fumiyo, *Kono sekai no katasumi ni, jô* (*In This Corner of the World*, I) (Tokyo: Futabasha, 2008a); Kouno Fumiyo, *Kono sekai no katasumi ni, chû* (*In This Corner of the World*, II) (Tokyo: Futabasha, 2008b); Kouno Fumiyo, *Kono sekai no katasumi ni, ge* (*In This Corner of the World*, III) (Tokyo: Futabasha, 2009); Kouno Fumiyo, *In This Corner of the World* (Los Angeles: Seven Seas Entertainment, 2017).
5. Yamashiro Tomoe, *Kono sekai no katasumi de* (Tokyo: Iwanami shinsho, 2007 [1965]).
6. Robbie Collin, "Tokyo Film Festival Review: In This Corner of the World Is a Dream-like Portrait of What Was Lost in the Blast of Hiroshima," *The Telegraph*

(online edition), October 28, 2016. https://www.telegraph.co.uk/films/0/in
-this-corner-of-the-world-review-a-dream-like-portrait-of-what/ (accessed
October 18, 2018).

7. Discussed in Takeuchi Miho, "Kouno Fumiyo's Hiroshima Manga: A Style-
Centered Attempt at Re-reading," *Kritika Kultura* 26 (2016): 243–57. https://
journals.ateneo.edu/ojs/index.php/kk/article/view/KK2016.02613 (accessed
October 18, 2018); DOI: http://dx.doi.org/10.13185/KK2016.02613.

8. Mark Schilling, "*In This Corner of the World*: Katabuchi's War Film Has a Human
Heart," *The Japan Times* (online edition), November 19, 2016. https://www
.japantimes.co.jp/culture/2016/11/16/films/film-reviews/corner-world
-katabuchis-war-film-human-heart/#.W9CGAy97HsE (accessed October 18,
2018).

9. Kouno Fumiyo and Nishijima Daisuke, "*Taidan: Katasumi yori ai o komete,*"
Eureka, December 2016: 39.

10. Hosoma Hiromichi, *Futatsu no "Kono sekai no katasumi ni": Manga, animêshon no
koe to dôsa* (Two versions of *In This Corner of the World*: Voice and movement in
manga and animation) (Tokyo: Seidosha, 2017), 160.

11. Kouno Fumiyo and Kayama Ryûshi, "Kouno Fumiyo Special Interview," in
Kouno Fumiyo, *Arigatô, uchi o mitsukete kurete* (Tokyo: Futabasha, 2017), 189.

12. Katalin Orbán, "A Language of Scratches and Stitches: The Graphic Novel
between Hyperreading and Print," *Critical Inquiry* (Spring 2014): 171.

13. Orbán, "A Language of Scratches and Stitches," 173.

14. Laura U. Marks, *Touch: Sensuous Theory and Multisensory Media* (Minneapolis:
University of Minnesota Press, 2002).

15. Natsume Fusanosuke, *Manga wa naze omoshiroi no ka? Sono hyôgen to bunpô*
(What makes manga interesting? Its expression and grammar) (Tokyo: NHK
shuppan, 1997); the article by Lukas R. A. Wilde in this issue.

16. Michael Taussig, "What Do Drawings Want?" *Culture, Theory and Critique* 50,
nos. 2–3 (2009): 271. DOI: 10.1080/14735780903240299.

17. John Berger, *Berger on Drawing*, edited by Jim Savage (London: Occasional Press,
2007), 3.

18. Cf. Takeuchi, "Kouno Fumiyo's Hiroshima Manga."

19. Kouno Fumiyo, "*Furui onna,*" *Washizumu* 19 (2006): 9–15.

20. Kouno, *In This Corner of the World*, 346.

21. Fukuma Yoshiaki, Yamaguchi Makoto, and Yoshimura Kazuma, "*Intabyû Kôno
Fumiyo: Hitaiken to manga hyôgen*" (Interview Kouno Fumiyo: Non-experience
and manga expression), in *Fukusû no "Hiroshima": Kioku no sengoshi to media
no rikigaku* (Multiple images of "Hiroshima": The postwar history of memory
and the dynamics of media), ed. Fukuma Yoshiaki, Yamaguchi Makoto, and
Yoshimura Kazuma (Tokyo: Seikyûsha, 2012), 380.

22. Fujitsu Ryôta, "*Intabyû bijutsu kantoku Hayashi Kôsuke*" (Interview with art director Hayashi Kôsuke], in *Kono sekai no katasumi ni: Gekijô anime kôshiki gaidobukku*

(In this corner of the world: Official guidebook to the animated movie) (Tokyo: Futabasha, 2016), 83.

23. Nancy Pedri, "Mixing Visual Media in Comics," *ImageTexT* 9, no. 2 (2017). http://www.english.ufl.edu/imagetext/ (accessed October 18, 2018).

24. Kouno, *In This Corner of the World*, 283.

25. Hosoma, *Futatsu no "Kono sekai no katasumi ni,"* 55.

26. *Kono sekai no katasumi ni seisaku iinkai*, ed., *Kono sekai no katasumi ni gekijô anime ekonte shû* (Storyboard collection for the animated movie In this corner of the world) (Tokyo: Futabasha, 2016), 487. In Japanese called "kine calligraph," according to Maria Roberta Novielli, *Floating Worlds: A Short History of Japanese Animation* (Boca Raton: Taylor & Francis, 2018), 47, who omits McLaren. Assistant unit director Nomura Kenta was in charge of this "cinegraphy animation," according to Hosoma, *Futatsu no "Kono sekai no katasumi ni,"* 70.

27. Launched in 1967 as a weekly magazine for *gekiga*, in 2004 it was turned into a bi-weekly. Gained renown for series such as *Lupin* by Monkey Punch, *Kozure ôkami* (Lone wolf and cub) by Koike Kazuo and Kojima Gôseki; and Usui Yoshito's *Crayon Shin-chan*.

28. Deborah Shamoon, *Passionate Friendship: The Aesthetics of Girls' Culture in Japan* (Honolulu: University of Hawai'i Press, 2012); Fujimoto Yukari, *Watashi no ibasho wa doko ni aru no? Shôjo manga ga utsusu kokoro no katachi* (Tokyo: Gakuyô Shobô, 2008 [1998]).

29. Giancarla Unser-Schutz, "Redefining Shôjo- and Shônen-Manga via Language Patterns," in *Shôjo Across Media: Exploring "Girl" Practices in Contemporary Japan*, ed. Jaqueline Berndt, Kazumi Nagaike, and Fusami Ogi (New York: Palgrave MacMillan, 2018), 72–73.

30. Kouno Fumiyo, *Town of Evening Calm, Country of Cherry Blossoms*, trans. Naoko Amemiya and Andy Nakatani (San Francisco: Last Gasp, 2006).

31. Horii Ken'ichirô, *"Dorama Kono sekai no katasumi ni wa sensô dorama toshite mitewa ikenai,"* gendai.ismedia.jp, https://gendai.ismedia.jp/articles/-/56642 (posted July 22, 2018) (accessed October 18, 2018).

32. Yoshimura Kazuma, *"Manga ni egakareta 'Hiroshima': Sono 'fûkei' kara yomitoku"* ("Hiroshima" as represented in manga: deciphered from the angle of its "landscape"), in *Fukusû no "Hiroshima*, 2012, 181–82.

33. Nakamura Tadashi, *"Manga ni okeru chikaku, ninshiki no hyôshô o megutte: Kôno Fumiyo no sakuhin o chûshin ni"* (On the representation of perception and cognition in comics, taking Kouno Fumiyo's works as example), in *Gendai shikaku hyôshô ni okeru mediateki shintai no kenkyû* (Studies on the mediatized body in contemporary visual representation), ed. Abe Kôji and Nakamura Tadashi (Yamagata: Yamagata University, Dept. of Humanities, 2015), 87.

34. Zoltan Kacsuk, "From "Game-like Realism" to "Imagination-oriented Aesthetic": Reconsidering Bourdieu's Contribution to Fan Studies in the Light of Japanese Manga and Otaku Theory," in *Kritika Kultura* 26 (2016): 274–92.

Manga Across Media

*Style Adapting to Form in the 1950s
and 1960s and in the Digital Age*

DALMA KÁLOVICS

If one refers to manga as a form of media, most people outside Japan think of paperbacks or so-called *tankôbon*. Nowadays, however, manga looks exactly the same across all print media, be it in big magazines, small paperbacks, or in even smaller pocketbooks. This is because the visual style of manga has been finely tuned to the materiality of books: manga is graphically composed to suit individual pages, panels are arranged within frames that echo the rectangular spaces of the single page and the double-spread, and panels, speech bubbles, and drawings establish a visual flow that guides the reader's gaze. However, while the paneling of manga and its other signature visual characteristics have been thoroughly researched in Japanese academia, and have been essential components of "how to draw manga" guides, the materiality of manga media is rarely discussed beyond the printed book. For many decades manga was bound to printed magazines and paperbacks of relatively unchanging size and format. As such, the materiality of manga was of secondary concern, but this has changed with the digital age.

It is not an exaggeration to say that manga is currently standing at a crossroad. The print runs of manga magazines have been declining for some time, and several magazines cease publication or move online every year. In contrast, digital comics have steadily risen over the past few years, and upon entering computer and smartphone screens the format of manga started to change. Aside from digital comics that use traditional panel layouts taken from print manga, a new type of comics composed in vertical strips has also appeared—so-called *webtoons*. The smartphone-optimized nature of webtoons has made researchers once again conscious of the materiality of manga, and that media does in fact determine how manga is presented.

Webtoons have been widely popular in Korea and China. And, although the manga industry in Japan is relatively resistant to big changes due to its sheer size and long-standing history, the popularity of webtoons, especially among young readers of the smartphone generation, suggests that even in Japan a shift is inevitable. Ushered in by digital comics, this formal shift seems enormous. But, looking back in history one can see that these changes are in line with manga's inherent ability to adapt to different types of media. To demonstrate this flexibility, I first examine manga across different media of the 1950s and 1960s, and then move on to examining the new comics of the digital age that show similar adaptability and publishing practices.

This article focuses on how the panel layout of manga has changed due to different sizes and forms of publishing media in Japanese and Korean comics. I intentionally do not consider other aspects such as the reading experience for several reasons. Visual style is usually considered in relation to the narrative, while the materiality of manga is rarely taken into account. However, as I introduce here, the form of manga's publishing media largely determines how panel layouts are structured. Also, I would like to avoid qualitative evaluation of the recent changes in manga style. It may be easy to interpret the recent shift toward vertical, scrolling formats as a "deterioration" of manga while ignoring the fact that this has been dictated by a change in the format of the media. For example, one might view the absence of double-spread compositions, which up until recently have been standard in manga, as a mark of inferiority, similar to what has happed in relation to Chinese comics.[1] However, this judgment does not take other factors into consideration, such as media or the state of the industry. Furthermore, beyond personal preferences, one's reading experience is largely determined by one's literacy of the medium. There are those who might find a manga just as enjoyable even without being aware of its complex visual techniques as well as those who, without a basic level of visual literacy, may be at a loss to navigate difficult compositions.

Terminology

For the purposes of this article, I understand the term *medium* to mean the tactile materiality of a product, like printed books, while I use *media* in a more abstract sense that incorporates production practices and publishing methods. Consequently, both major magazines and rental manga paperbacks are the same medium, i.e., printed books, but they are different media due to their separate sites of production and circulation, as well as the social circumstances of their main readership, like age, status and finances.

Likewise, digital comics use electronic data framed by computers and smartphones as their medium. I distinguish between traditional-format digital comics and scrolling-format "webtoons" as different media, although the borderline between their sites of publication and audiences is less distinct. Since digital comics are a result of the media convergence between the traditional comic format and the technology of the internet, it can also be said the difference between traditional-format digital comics and scrolling-format webtoons lies in their respective levels of convergence. Also, for the sake of clarity, I differentiate between *digital manga*, meaning Japanese traditional-format comics published on the internet, and *webtoons*, scrolling-format comics on the internet, while I use *digital comics* as a broader term to refer to any type of comics published online.

Manga Adapting to Media in the 1950s–60s

Currently, the structure of manga does not change regardless of its publishing media, whether in big magazines or small tankôbon. However, in the 1950s and 1960s the appearance of comics was adjusted to fit the media. Its format and related publishing practices determined the visual style of comics, the structure of their narratives and the flow of the storytelling. Graphics and storytelling are closely related, but in this article, I focus solely on the visual aspects of manga without addressing how different publishing practices affected the structure and tempo of manga narratives.

In the following section, I introduce manga of different publication sites in the 1950s and 1960s, as well as manga crossing over from one media to another. Although the visual style of manga is built from a variety of elements, for the sake of simplicity I focus mainly on the number of tiers in which panels were arranged. As my main field of research is the media history of 1960s *shôjo* manga I use shôjo manga examples within this article, but my observations are applicable to other genres.

TWO MANGA MARKETS

As recorded in many manga histories, in the 1950s and 1960s two manga markets existed next to each other: rental manga by small publishers versus mainstream magazines by big publishing houses, and the layout of manga differed between these two media. Rental manga appeared in Japan around 1953 as a form of cheap entertainment during the poor economy that followed the Korean War (1950–53).[2] Rental manga was most popular in the 1950s but gradually lost importance in favor of major weekly magazines. By the end of the 1960s, rental manga had almost completely disappeared.

Rental books, released by minor specialized publishers, were available in downtown stores often tied to candy shops and public baths. Rental manga was offered at a low price that even children could afford. Purchasing a rental paperback cost 130 yen, but it could be borrowed nightly for a mere 10 yen.[3] Rental publishers gave opportunities to emerging artists, who could not have debuted in major magazines, and the media became an incubator for new talent, which would eventually be sapped away by mainstream manga. Although rental manga did not pay as much as larger publishers, artists valued these smaller enterprises for their relative freedom of expression and the ability to publish long, standalone narratives, as opposed to the short installments of magazines.[4]

In the beginning, rental manga was published in hard cover B6 (128 × 182 mm) books,[5] but by the end of the 1950s the format had changed to A5 (148 × 210 mm) with soft covers.[6] Rental manga was originally dedicated to a single narrative, but at the end of the 1950s anthologies were launched to rival the success of mainstream magazines.[7] I have only been able to examine soft cover A5-sized rental books, and these used almost exclusively a three-tier panel layout, occasionally reaching four tiers.

Children's magazines by major publishers were first printed in A5 format, and the current, bigger B5 size (182 × 257 mm) became common in the 1950s, when the readers' focus shifted toward visual entertainment. At first, manga comprised only a small part of magazine content, but the ratio of graphic narratives gradually increased. In the Shueisha monthly *Shôjo Book,* manga content rose from 10 percent in the early 1950s to 30 percent by the end of the decade. Installments were initially quite short—usually around eight pages— but the length of episodes grew to 10–15 pages by the end of the 1950s.

Manga in the larger B5 format of children's magazines was standardized to include four tiers, but there were smaller and bigger formats in use as well. The extra editions (*zôkan*) of *Shôjo Book* were released in A5 size and panels within were arranged accordingly in three tiers, just like in A5 rental books. *Ribon Comics* was published in the even smaller B6 format, where paneling was also composed in three tiers. At the same time, the extra editions of *Nakayoshi* were released in A4 format (210 × 297 mm), and this allowed paneling in five tiers. In the case of small inserts paneling was arranged in three tiers or less.

While magazines themselves were low on manga content, additional comics were released in freebie booklets *(bessatsu furoku)* distributed with the magazines, and these could reach 100 pages whereas monthly magazines were typically only around 200–250 pages. Usually, the magazine published the first eight pages as an installment, which then continued in the furoku. However, sometimes furoku contained all new narratives.

They came in various formats (B5, A5, B6, A6, B7, etc.), and this had an impact on the paneling of manga. Generally, three-tier paneling was employed, but in tiny furoku even two-tier layouts can be found, like in Higashiura Mitsuo's *Osuzu-chan (Little Suzu)* published in an A6-sized (105 × 148 mm) *Shôjo Club* furoku in 1957. And notably, in the B5 square format (182 × 205 mm) booklets of *Ribon*, while the panels were arranged into three tiers the square page dimensions make the layouts seem wider.

Manga across Different Media in the 1950s–60s

The works cited up until now are all examples of a single media per narrative. However, long running series were habitually published both in magazines and furoku, adjusting paneling to the size of the media. But what happens when these differently structured parts are published together? Publishing of collected books under the specific label now known as tankôbon did not start until the second half of the 1960s, but that does not mean that there were no compilations at all. Before mainstream publishers began releasing their serializations in book form, rental publishers occasionally compiled magazine installments, as they already specialized in releasing standalone books. Like rental books, these paperbacks were too expensive for the average consumer, therefore they ended up in rental circulation as well.

An example of a rental compilation is Watanabe Masako's *Yamabiko shôjo (Mountain girl)*. The series was originally published between 1957 and 1959 in *Shôjo Book* with a four-tier panel layout and three tiers in the smaller furoku. Rental publisher Wakagi Shobô collected the material and released it in six hardcover volumes between 1958 and 1959. The two differently paneled layouts of the manga had to be unified for the tankôbon edition, thus the material was edited to fit the standard three tiers of rental manga by dividing the panels of one magazine page in two (Figures 1 and 2).

The opposite can be observed in Chiba Tetsuya's *1, 2, 3 to 4, 5 no Roku (1, 2, 3 and 4, 5's Roku)*, which was serialized in the A5 furoku of Kodansha's *Shôjo Club*

Figure 1. Watanabe Masako, *Yamabiko shôjo* (Mountain girl), *Shôjo Book*, 1958, 1.

Figure 2. Watanabe Masako, *Yamabiko shôjo 1* (Mountain girl 1), *Home-sha*, 2001, 106–7.

utilizing three tiers in 1962, and the same paneling was retained in the paperbacks by rental publisher Kinransha. From 1966–1967, however, the series was once again published in the B5-sized magazine *Bessatsu Shôjo Friend* as a collected edition *(sôshûhen)*, in 50+ page portions each month. For this release, the manga was altered radically to make it fit the standard four-tier layout of magazines—most pages were cut, panels were rearranged and smaller panels were enlarged with additional drawings to create a new manuscript.

While such extreme examples are rare, in general manga were freely edited across media. When the current model of tankôbon publishing started in the second half of the 1960s, some editing was necessary to turn magazine publications into paperback. Some of these can still be observed, like replacing advertisements with extra panels or illustrations. Furthermore, repeat contents in the beginning of an episode, summaries and introductions of characters were also removed to create a continuous story. However, this often meant that the position of pages changed and double-page spreads were torn apart, disrupting the original flow. For instance, in the magazine serialization of Mizuno Hideko's *Venus no yume (Dream of Venus)*, the flow of the double-page spread naturally guided the reader's gaze with the placement of the full-body illustration. However, in the tankôbon release the page ended up on the opposite side, causing the full-body shot to obstruct the flow. The same displacement of pages happened simply by connecting installments with even and uneven page numbers, which was not rare, as serializations were not yet created with a paperback release in mind.

Such editing was only possible because neither editors nor artists had begun to place importance on the double-page spreads. Since then, composing manga across the two pages of the double-page spread has become standard. From this standpoint, one might conclude that manga publishing in the 1960s was not fully developed yet. However, I suggest regarding this centrality of the single page as just one possible approach to manga and one that has eventually reemerged in the digital age, where mediums like e-book readers and smartphones use the single page as a basic unit of display.

Decades of Fixed Style and a New Shift

With the birth of the manga industry at the end of the 1960s, the flexibility of manga fell into oblivion. With the improvement of living standards in Japan major magazines were able to achieve overwhelming success while rental manga gradually lost importance and perished. The concept of furoku manga did not disappear entirely, but it faded as magazines focused almost entirely on comics. The publication pattern of magazines to tankôbon, still present today, became commonplace in the 1970s and this led to a fixed visual style in manga. There was no need to adjust differently structured layouts anymore, and every manga publishing media ended up shrinking or enlarging the same visuals depending on its size. Manga did not adapt to different media for many decades, which made it easy for one to assume that what is seen in magazines and tankôbon is the "one and only" manga style, but this status quo has been challenged by the digital age and the rise of digital comics, that came to rival print manga.

The print market for manga has been in decline since the mid-1990s, and print runs of manga magazines have been steadily decreasing. For example, the bestselling *Weekly Shônen Jump* achieved a record print run of 6.53 million at the end of 1994 with the 1995/3-4 double issue, but that figure has since dropped below 2 million in the first quarter of 2017, standing at 1.76 million in the first quarter of 2018.[8] Notably, *Weekly Shônen Jump* is the only manga magazine to exceed the one-million-copy threshold.

News about manga magazines ceasing publication has also become commonplace: 2018 has seen the end of long-running monthlies like *Bessatsu Hana to Yume* (since 1977), *YOU* (since 1982) and *Monthly Comic Ryû* (since 1979) among others. The shortfall of manga magazines has been balanced by tankôbon sales, but even those have been on the decline. In 2016, the sales of printed comic books and magazines altogether decreased by 9.3 percent; manga magazines alone decreased by 12.9 percent and paperbacks decreased by 7.4 percent.[9]

In contrast, the digital market has been on the rise since the 2000s, achieving overwhelming success. In 2008, the digital comic market was worth 25.5 billion yen,[10] and in eight years it increased to 149.1 billion yen.[11] In 2016, the digital manga market increased by 27.5 percent; digital comic books alone increased by 27.1 percent and digital manga magazines by 55 percent.[12] Interestingly, comics have been the pillar of digital publishing in Japan owning 76.5 percent of the market.[13] The market share of digital comics with 149.1 billion yen is still lagging behind the 296.3 billion yen of printed manga (Figure 3),[14] but the reach of digital might be even bigger, as some comic portals offer contents for free.

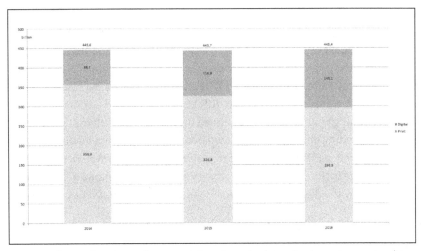

Figure 3. The market share of print and digital comics (paperbacks and magazines) in 2016, Source: *Shuppan Kagaku Kenkyûjo* ed., *2017-ban Shuppan Shihyô Nenpô* (Tokyo: Zenkoku Shuppan Kyôkai, 2017), 212.

Japanese Digital Manga

Although Japan's print market for comics is the biggest in the world, with the digital age manga came to be offered on computer screens and small screen flip phones since 2003, and for that its form had to be edited. While the digital manga market in Japan has been phone-centric since its beginning (in 2008, the ratio of PC to cell phone comics was around 1:9),[15] digital manga has been consistently offered in PC format. Because PCs are able to display manga largely like they appear in printed matter, transferring the page to the computer screen did not have much of an impact on the aesthetics of manga. Looking at major websites offering digital manga such as Comic Cmoa (https://www.cmoa.jp/), Booklive (https://booklive.jp/), and Ebookjapan (http://www.ebookjapan.jp/ebj/), all use a double-page-spread page view by default to display manga.

In contrast, the traditional manga format had to be edited for phone screens that predated the smartphone era, as cellphone technology at that time could not accommodate the same layout as paper-based media, nor was it suitable for transferring high quality images. A panel-by-panel view was offered for tiny cellphone screens, for example, through the collaboration of manga publisher Shogakukan and digital contents distributor NTT Solmare, but this required scanning the print versions of manga and cutting individual pages into panels to make them suitable for cellphone viewing.[16] Another, less labor intensive solution was the creation of a viewer for cellphones released in 2003 by software maker Celsys called *Comic Surfing*, where readers could slide across a traditional manga page by viewing only part of a page at a time and scrolling to the next; this technology was adopted by the application *Bunko Viewer* by cellphone operator NTT Docomo.[17]

These cellphone-oriented formats gradually disappeared with the rising ubiquity of smartphones. Nowadays, smartphones have large enough screens to display manga pages, albeit only one page at a time, making the single page view default on digital manga smartphone applications. Be it digitized or born-digital material, contemporary online manga by major publishers utilizes the same aesthetics as print publications; the only difference being that on smartphones the single page became the basic unit of manga, thus double-page-spread compositions may lose importance in the future, but this should not be seen as a deterioration of manga. As mentioned above, at least until the 1960s, the basic unit of Japanese manga was the single page, as suggested by the edits for paperback releases that time, and if manga publishing shifts to smartphones, which can only display a single page at a time, composing double-spread will be superfluous. Furthermore, there have been comic markets that have been mostly single-page-centric in print too: although receiving much influence from Japanese manga, Chinese comics, having been published in many different formats, have never developed a consciousness of double-page spreads as seen in Japanese comics, but neither artists nor readers seem to be bothered by this.

Although online manga endangers some aspects of print manga, like double-page-spread compositions, the traditional-format digital manga industry has presented itself as a savior of print manga magazines: currently, it is commonplace for publishers to move their series online if the print magazine ceases publication, sometimes even under the name of the original magazine. All three of the previously mentioned magazines that ceased publication in 2018 resorted to this solution. The shift to digital is not complete, though, because popular online serializations are still published in print paperbacks.

There has also been a burgeoning of born-digital manga magazines. Some of these are available for free on dedicated websites like *Shōnen Jump+* (https://shonenjumpplus.com/since 2014), and others on portals like *Pixiv Comic* (https://comic.pixiv.net/ since 2012) where products by several publishers are released for free until a paperback is compiled. Digital manga, including magazines and standalone serializations, has also been made available for purchase on big e-book portals like Cmoa and Booklive.

KOREAN WEBTOONS

While digital manga exclusively uses the traditional style of manga, another type of digital comic with new stylistics and publishing practices has been gaining ground in Japan: webtoons. Even though computer screens can accommodate traditional manga pages, this desktop format is still optimized for the materiality of printed books. Because content on the internet is accessible across multiple platforms, a comic form like webtoons are optimized for the web and expectedly look different, utilizing the vertical scroll inherent to navigating websites. A relatively new area of English-language discourse, webtoons are garnering academic attention in a range of dimensions: as a product of media convergence and as a transmedia storytelling format; to highlight their stylistic differences from print comics; or for their rapid growth in Korea, as well as international success.

Webtoons (also called "scroll comics" and *tate sukurôru* [vertical scroll] in Japan) emerged at the end of the 1990s in Korea, when paper-based comic magazines crumbled due to a national financial crisis. Many amateur artists started to publish on their own websites by lining up single images with small pieces of text inserted in between. But, as consumers adopted computer "mouses" that featured wheels, webtoons came to be created in a long, vertical scroll.[18] This new comic form was soon offered on big portals, and webtoon-centric websites proliferated.[19] While traditional-format comics, both print and digital (called *manhwa* for the sake of differentiation), still exist in Korea, nowadays most comics are published in a vertical-scrolling layout on web portals.

As opposed to traditional manhwa, webtoons are usually created in color, and composed in a long vertical strip, where only one or a few panels are visible at once, and the reader must scroll down to read further. The size of the screen determines how much is visible at a time, but scroll comics often use wide *gutters*, or the margins between panels, ensuring the screen will not be crowded with too much content. Webtoons have been regarded as a realization of Scott McCloud's "infinite canvas,"[20] albeit in a limited way, since webtoons have a fixed width, and though vertically long, they are not endless.

The paneling of webtoons was quite simple at first, and this was likely because the amateur artists making them were unfamiliar with the conventions of creating comics.[21] While simple paneling became customary, cinematic techniques and multilayered compositions have been frequently used in webtoons, and the more prominent gutters have gained attention for their capacity to aid in narrating the story. Although it might seem like images are simply lined up one after another in webtoons, the drawings, panels and speech bubbles are all carefully composed to create a wavelike visual flow that guides the gaze of the reader.

Some artists have even added sound to their comics. For example, when scrolling through the horror anthology *Sorane no hanabi* (*Sorane's firework,* 2014-16) on Comico, readers encounter moving panels and scary sounds or music to amplify the mood, though these features are only available on the smartphone app. Sounds and movement seem to fit genres like horror the best, and adding this kind of interactivity to webtoons has not yet become mainstream. Adding other media increases the workload and costs of creating comics, and readers also potentially need additional equipment, like headphones, to enjoy multimedia comics. Therefore, most webtoons can be thought of as simply web-optimized comics.

Webtoons were disseminated to other countries via online comic portals of Korean origin, and gained popularity quickly. In 2016, the almost $32.5 million (USD) export of the Korean comic industry (manhwa and webtoons altogether) exceeded the $6.5 million (USD) import by a substantial margin. The largest foreign markets for Korean comics are Europe, followed by Japan, Southeast Asia, and the United States.[22] Although Korean comics have been promoted as a national brand, the scroll format soon lost its specificity to Korean pop culture and has since become a universal form for digital comics around the world.

WEBTOONS IN JAPAN

Japan's first smartphone application to publish Korean webtoons, Naver Webtoons, debuted in 2011. The first application with additional website, Comico, was launched in 2013 by NHN Comico, a subsidiary of the Korean NHN Entertainment, and has been publishing Japanese and translated Korean webtoons, albeit the origins of the comics are usually not stated. Several Japanese webtoons have already become hits, like *ReLIFE* by Yayoisô (2013–18, adapted to anime in 2016 and live action movie in 2017) and *How to Keep a Mummy* by Utsugi Kakeru (*Miira no kaikata,* 2014–present, adapted to anime in 2018). Several apps of Korean ownership publish webtoons in Japan currently, but other than Comico only Line Manga (https://manga.line.me/) recruits Japanese talent.

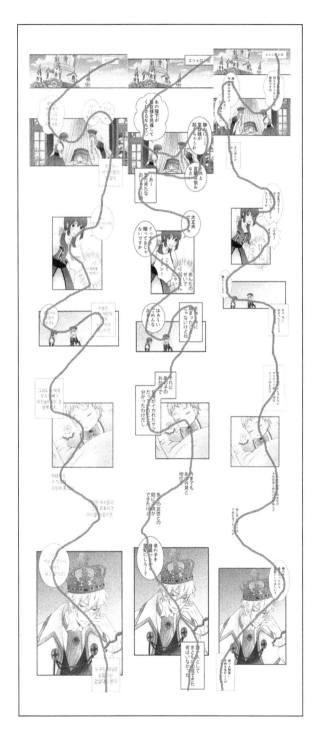

Figure 4. Different flow of text and images in the Korean (left) and Japanese (middle and right) versions of *Daughter of the Emperor*, chapter 1 by Yunsul & Rino (KakaoPage, 2015; Comico, 2017; Piccoma, 2017).

At this point, it is wise to address how Korean webtoons are adapted in Japan. Although it may seem like scroll comics can be consumed regardless of an original reading order, Japanese adaptations employ some editing like the practice of "flipping" and shifting panels and speech bubbles to achieve a more natural flow for Japanese readers. For *Koisuru apuri—Love alarm (Love app—Love alarm)*, the Japanese translation of *Joh ahamyeon ullineun (Love alarm,* 2014–18) by Chon Kye-young, the flow was shifted by flipping and moving speech bubbles. Unsurprisingly, the Korean paperback version was wholly flipped to adjust the reading order when the webtoon was released in book form in Japan.

Even more intriguing is the popular Korean series *Daughter of the Emperor (Hwangjeui oedongttal,* 2015–present) by Yunsul and Rino, that has been adapted by two Japanese webtoon portals, Piccoma (https://piccoma.com /web/) and Comico as *Kôtei no hitori musume.* Both publishers edit the material: Comico is less drastic, it changes the flow mostly by shifting speech bubbles, while Piccoma also flips panels and uses a bigger gutter, in general (Figure 4). Surprisingly, the translated paperbacks published by Kadokawa retain the Korean reading order, which is often remarked by Amazon reviewers as a problem. While Western readers have long gotten used to the "opposite" reading order of manga, Japanese readers are less tolerant in that regard, thus the editing of scroll-format comics across cultures will probably persist.

Similarities between the Rental Market and Webtoon Publishing

Although webtoons are a new media, the publishing practices and industry behind it mirror several aspects of the 1950s–60s rental manga market:

Cheap pricing and the ability to rent
Small scale of publishers
Innovation and experimentation
Provides opportunity for emerging talent
Underpayment of artists
Lack of preservation
Difficulties of academic research

In this section, I address these points and organize them around two major concerns: publishing and research.

Webtoons started out as personal projects by artists who made their content available for free. Since the media has been commercialized, episodes have been offered for a small price that might be comparable with the fee of rental manga. A renting system is in use as well: both Comico and Piccoma allow readers to view older installments of series for free for a few days using a rental "ticket" that would recharge over the course of a day after usage. While traditional-format digital manga is hardly cheaper than the paper version, a renting system exists there as well. For instance, Renta and Cmoa offer partial access to their catalogs for two to three days for half or sometimes two-thirds of the normal rental price.

Just like rental manga, webtoons have been released by small publishers and portals initially not well versed in comic making. Personal publishing projects were not restricted by editorial directives and, although publishers and editors later became involved, webtoons are still considered freer in terms of their creative license than print magazines by major companies. As in the past, the relative creative freedom of the small-scale producers allow for some experimentation, thus one can find works with a wide range of visual styles and themes. Webtoon publishers also provide opportunities to emerging artists who might not yet be good enough for a magazine debut. Most webtoon sites maintain a "challenge page" where amateurs can submit their work, and, if their comic gains enough online support, then it moves forward to a publishing debut. Currently, debuting in webtoons is considered far easier than publishing in a print magazine.[23]

However, webtoons do not only share positive traits with rental manga. Because webtoons are published by small companies, artists receive relatively small pay for their work.[24] In addition, some webtoon publishers have also been exposed to practice exploitative behaviors towards artists. In early 2018, several reports surfaced about Korean webtoon publisher Lezhin mistreating and blacklisting artists. Furthermore, the company received harsh criticism for the unfair split of sales and penalty fees in the case that an artist could not make their deadline.[25]

In relation to webtoons there are also concerns regarding research. It has been often discussed that digital data is more fleeting than paper-based publications due to the threat that in the span of only a few years file formats, reading devices, and the current standards of display technologies might become obsolete. In the case of digital comics, however, disappearing content is an imminent danger. Unlike printed matter, which is difficult to erase entirely once out and circulating in the market, access to digital manga can disappear any time. Digital works have been taken off websites due to expired contracts or disagreements with artists, and such comics are likely lost forever. Webtoons and digital manga are not institutionally archived yet, but with the growing number of digital publications the issue of digital archiving needs to be addressed urgently. This situation is quite similar to the age of rentals, when practices around manga archiving were still lacking and focused only on mainstream magazines, thereby effacing the record of many rental publications.

Due to material loss, research on digital comics may face difficulties in the future, but in Japan there is yet another negative issue shared with the rental manga industry: the lack of recorded publication dates. In the 1960s, rental manga did not mark release dates, so books could be circulated for a long time. Unless there are academic or journalistic records, it is extremely difficult now to find out when certain narratives were published, and only the random signatures of artists might give a hint.

Online comics might lack release dates for a similar reason, but in digital manga it is also related to special publishing practices. Materials are released on several platforms, but usually there is one privileged website that publishes the content ahead of others by several weeks. Afterward, when a digital manga is released in print, the original publication date of the installments is either not recorded or only the publishing label of the online magazine is recorded without a date. Although in the case of the privileged websites there is an initial release date to record, this is currently not practiced. Also, because release dates are usually not recorded on most digital manga sites either, it is difficult to find out when respective narratives were published. In the case of short story collections, several years might pass between the initial online release and the print release, making it crucial to note the original publication date of each narrative on the colophon page of the paperback.

Manga Adapts to Media Once Again

With the digital age manga started to adapt to media once again: traditional comics were cut for cellphones and web-optimized scroll comics were born. Although it might seem like webtoons are a new media unrelated to traditional manga, there is a close connection between them in that the adaptability of manga comes into play even more. Popular webtoons are eventually republished as traditional manga paperbacks in both Korea and Japan, and the visual structure of those comics have to be changed fundamentally. Although less conspicuous, there have also been examples of adapting traditional comics to scroll-format layouts.

Adapting traditional-layout comics to scrolling layouts is practiced in Korea and China, and applies to both domestic and foreign comics. Niyama's *My Dearest Cop* (*Boku no omawarisan*, 2017) was originally released as a traditional digital manga in Japan, then for the Korean webtoon portal Lezhin the pages were cut and panels were rearranged to create a vertical scroll. This type of editing is still unusual in Japan, though not unprecedented: Renta published a scroll version of *Tweeting Love Birds* (*Chuchun ga chun*, 2009-10) by Yamamoto Kotetsuko, where the monochrome pages were also colored to fit the webtoon trends.

Satoru's *Ore ga . . . yuri?!* (*A boy . . . in yuri?!*, 2015-16), a Japanese digital manga in color, provides a rare opportunity to compare Korean and Japanese scrolling layouts of the same material. Their structures are quite similar, and notably the Korean version did not edit the reading order. But there are several differences like the thickness of the gutter, the background or the adaptation of the full body shot—retaining its overlaid nature in the Japanese version while creating a new panel with a background in the Korean one. Overall, while scroll comics have their own grammar, adapting from paperback layout to scroll is relatively easy.

Still, adaptation generally happens from scroll to paperback, proving that print manga publications are still relevant. When webtoons are released as a print paperback, the vertical-scroll of panels has to be turned into a traditional panel construction. Aforementioned *ReLIFE* was published in print in 2014, and while panels of similar sizes were placed one after another in the webtoon version, these panels were organized into a book layout by changing their sizes and positions.

Remarkably, the paneling of paperbacks created from webtoons is rather simple. Printed manga and web-optimized scrolls are two structurally different media, and adapting scrolling layouts to paperback formats is a particularly difficult task, as existing panels of potentially different sizes need to be tessellated into a working page layout, like puzzle pieces. The paneling of traditional comics is a complex system, where the position, size, and interrelation of panels, the gutter or the layering all bear importance. It is almost impossible to create a complex layout out of existing panels adhering to every rule of traditional paneling, thus usually simple layouts are favored.

ReLIFE is an example of a typical design solution, but there are even simpler solutions. In the case of Nazee's Korean *Ppul ppul ppul ppul* (*Horns*, 2016) scrolls were just planted onto the book pages without much editing. For the Korean *Ius saram* (*Neighbor*, 2008) by Kang Pul (also cited by *The Comic Journal*) two different print versions exist, but neither seem to care about maintaining the flow of the narrative. The 2009 version simply put two scrolls next to each other on the page; the 2012 version adjusted the paneling to create a visual rhythm, but even here the tension of the scene is robbed by placing a panel that reveals part of the pending action on the same page as those panels building up the tension in advance of that action (Figure 5). There have been attempts to create slightly more complex paneling by using overlaid images in Lee Narae's *Bloody Sweet* (*Honey Blood*, 2014–17), but this is quite rare.

To avoid difficulties in editing scrolls for tankôbon formats, some artists work with a traditional layout even though the first publication happens in scroll format. Korean artist Park Ji-yeon did not expect a book release for her first webtoon, *Momentum* (2015–16), and afterward she struggled with creating a traditional layout. Therefore, anticipating a subsequent print release, she created her next webtoon series, *Wolf in the House* (since 2017), with a traditional layout and then edited them into scrolls for the web release.[26] This is an unusual method, but it seems as long as print paperbacks are still being published the need to create manga in traditional layouts will not disappear.

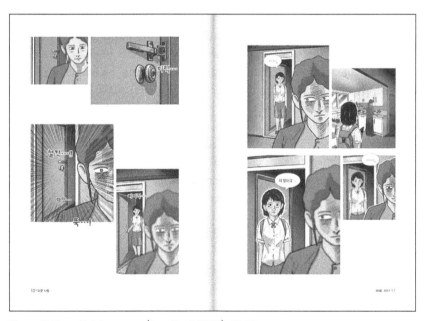

Figure 5. Kang Pul, *Ius saram* (Jaemijuui, 2012), 10–11.

Possibilities for the Future

Over the years there have been many Korean artists who switched from traditional comics to scrollable webtoons after the market shift, like *Love Alarm*'s Chon Kye-young, but the opposite also happens. Since the cultures of traditional print comics and webtoons seem to be closely intertwined, this might have consequences for the traditional manga form in the future, like a shift to simpler paneling as in the example of a scroll artist like Park Ji-yeon creating traditional manga layouts would suggest.

CTK debuted with the scroll comic *Coffin Jackson* (*Jaegseunui gwan*, 2015–16) in Korea, then drew a traditional style manga for the Japanese publisher Libre, *On Doorstep* (2016–17), which was released digitally for free on Pixiv Comic with a subsequent paperback. In the beginning, CTK was trying to make use of the whole page, and while her layout was not overly complex, she used overlaid and irregularly shaped panels. Yet, starting with chapter 3 in the narrative she changed the paneling to a very simple layout featuring the most basic panels, leaving a thick outer frame, and this style was retained for the rest of the serialization.

CTK's example brings to mind the simple paneling strategies of publishers adapting paperbacks from scrolls, as well as the simple layouts generally seen in rental manga. The connection between rental manga artists and the example of CTK might be that in both cases a lack of experience was a significant factor. Rental manga artists were often literally beginners at their craft, and while CTK was no beginner as an artist it can be assumed she was not used to drawing manga in the traditional way and quickly fell back into a habit of simple paneling that may stem from her scrolling-format origins.

In both cases, the key issue is the literacy of artists. Similar to the past when the practices of different media like rental manga or major magazines in turn changed the practices of artists and publishers, in the future we may also see changes in manga due to the influence of webtoons. The more artists whose practices originate with scroll comics enter the print market the bigger the impact there will be on traditional manga. The same is true for new readers who grow up only reading webtoons; they might not gain the literacy to read traditional, 'complicated' panel layouts, and this in turn could make traditional manga shift toward a standard of simpler structure.

Conclusion

As I mentioned in the beginning, manga is standing at a historical crossroad. The birth of a new manga media owed its innovations to the evolution of digital technology in tandem with the steady decline of the traditional manga market, and leaves no doubt that significant changes are bound to happen. But, these changes might be faster or slower depending on the markets and cultural traditions of their respective countries. Webtoons became popular in Korea because the necessary technological conditions (high-speed internet, wide adoption of computers and smartphones) already existed in the country, and its print comic market never prospered as much as its Japanese counterpart.

In Japan, print manga has a long-established tradition, and despite its declining state the market is still huge. Therefore, major publishers are less likely to drastically change their practices, and this is also true for older readers. Remarkably, the 2018 conference of the Japan Society for Studies in Cartoons and Comics in Kyoto (June 23–24, 2018) picked "Manga of the Digital Age" as its main theme, but only Chinese and Korean speakers addressed the topic of webtoons. Paradoxically, less and less Japanese children are reading traditional manga and thus are less apt than previous generations to understand its form. At the same time, more and more young readers end up consuming webtoons easily available on their smartphones, thus a shift in Japanese manga culture is inevitable.[27]

However, as I attempted to introduce through publishing practices of the 1950s to the 1960s, adapting to different media is very much in the nature of manga despite the fact that this has been somewhat forgotten over time. From this point of view, the birth of webtoons can be seen as a natural development in which artists are doing nothing more than making use of a new type of canvas and creating comics most suitable for it. This is not that different from creating specific panel layouts for every print book size, but the impact is bigger, as print media was effectively replaced by electronic media.

Born from the convergence of old comic formats and new technologies, webtoons are still a new media, and the future development of the format is something to look forward to. Although not touched upon in this paper, it is noteworthy to mention that the Chinese market has already embraced the webtoon format, adding its own flavor to the media. However, as stated by roundtable speaker Koo Bon Won at the same Kyoto conference, webtoons are surely not the end of the road. Nobody knows what new technologies and media will emerge and become mainstream hereafter, but comics will likely adapt to them just as they adapted to the Web.

....

Dalma Kálovics is a researcher at Yokote Masuda Manga Museum, Yokote City, Akita Prefecture, Japan. She received her PhD in manga from Kyoto Seika University, Japan, in 2019. She has been researching 1960s shôjo manga by conducting magazine research focused on *Weekly Margaret*, during which she became interested in the interrelation of manga with other media as well as the materiality of media.

....

Notes

1. Xu Muyun, "Manga no "mihiraki"—Keisai media o chûshin ni" ("Double-spread" in manga—From the perspective of publishing media), Kyoto Seika Daigaku Kokusai Kenkyû Center Nenji Hôkokusho 2017 (Annual Report 2017 Kyoto Seika University International Manga Research Center, 2017), 43.

2. Nakano Haruyuki, *Manga sangyôron* (Theory of the manga industry) (Tokyo: Chikuma Shobô, 2007[2004]), 55.

3. Naiki Toshio, "Kashihon manga" (Rental manga), in Naiki, *Manga no Shôwa shi: Shôwa 20 nen-55 nen* (Tokyo: Random House Kodansha, 2008), 44.

4. Nakano, *Manga sangyôron*, 59.

5. Kibi Yoshito, "Shôjotachi no yume no yukue: Shôjo manga no sekai" (Where do girls' dreams go: The world of shôjo manga), in *Kashihon manga RETURNS* (Rental manga RETURNS), ed. Kashihon Manga Kenkyûkai (Tokyo: Poplar Publishing, 2006), 178.

6. Yonezawa Yoshihiro, *Kodomo no Shôwa-shi: Shônen manga no sekai I* (A children's history of the Shôwa period: The world of shônen manga I) (Tokyo: Heibonsha, 1996), 110.

7. Kitamura Jirô, "Shinjin mangaka no tôryûmon datta Wakagi Shobô" (The gateway to success for young artists: Wakagi Shobô), in Yonezawa, *Kodomo no Shôwa-shi: Shôjo manga no sekai I*, 135.

8. JMPS Nihon Zasshi Kyôkai, "Insatsu busû kôkyô" (Announcement of print numbers), https://www.j-magazine.or.jp/user/printed/index/40/14 (accessed June 7, 2018).

9. Shuppan Kagaku Kenkyûjo, ed., *2017-ban Shuppan Shihyô Nenpô* (Annual report on the publishing industry 2017) (Tokyo: Zenkoku Shuppan Kyôkai, 2017), 212.

10. Nakano Haruyuki, *Manga shinkaron: Kontentsu bijinesu wa manga kara umareru!* (The evolution of manga: Contents business is born from manga!) (Tokyo: Blues Interactions, 2009), 19.

11. *2017-ban Shuppan Shihyô Nenpô*, 212.

12. *2017-ban Shuppan Shihyô Nenpô*, 212.

13. *2017-ban Shuppan Shihyô Nenpô*, 283.

14. *2017-ban Shuppan Shihyô Nenpô*, 212.

15. Nakano, *Manga shinkaron*, 184.

16. ITmedia Mobile, "Komikku wa keitai de tanoshimu jidai ni" (The time has come to enjoy comics on cell phones), http://www.itmedia.co.jp/mobile/articles /0504/06/news035.html (accessed June 7, 2018).

17. ITmedia Mobile, "'Kami o dejitaru-ka' no, sono saki e—Serushisu" (Beyond "turning paper into digital"—Celsys), https://www.itmedia.co.jp/mobile /articles/0406/15/news082.html (accessed June 7, 2018).

18. Park Su-In, "Kankoku no Uebutûn" (Korean webtoon), in *Kokusai Manga Kenkyû 3 Nikkan Manga Kenkyû* (*Global Studies of Manga Vol. 3 Japanese-Korean Manga Studies*), ed. Jaqueline Berndt, Yamanaka Chie, Leem Hye Jeong, 228–29 (Kyoto: Kyoto Seika University International Manga Research Center, 2013).

19. Jin, *Communication Research and Practice*, 198–99.

20. Scott McCloud, *Reinventing Comics: How Imagination and Technology are Revolutionizing an Art Form* (New York: Perennial, 2010), 222.

21. Park, *Kokusai Manga Kenkyû 3*, 228–29.

22. Korea Creative Content Agency Industry Promotion Policy Headquarters, *Manhwa saneobbaegseo 2017* (Graphic Novel Industry White Paper 2017) (Seoul: Korea Creative Content Agency, 2018), 2–3.

23. Park, *Kokusai Manga Kenkyû 3*, 238.

24. Jin, *Communication Research and Practice*, 201–2.

25. *The Magic Rain*, "What's Up With Lezhin? A Summary," http://www.themagic rain.com/2018/02/whats-up-with-lezhin-a-summary/ (accessed June 13, 2018); The Mnt, "When All That Glitters Is Not Gold: Webtoon Creators vs. Lezhin Comics". (accessed June 13, 2018).

26. Park Ji-yeon, *Wolf in the House*, Season 1 Epilogue (Seoul: Lezhin Entertainment, 2018), https://www.lezhin.com/en/comic/wolf_en/e1.

27. AppMarketingLabo, "*Apuri de yomeba subete muryô, soredemo tankôbon ga ureru riyû. Manga apuri 'Comico' ni kiku, sumaho jidai no manga kontentsu*" (You can read it for free on the app, but paperbacks still sell. We ask manga app Comico about the manga contents of the smartphone generation), http://appmarketing labo.net/comico/ (accessed 28 June, 2018).

Emerging "2.5-dimensional" Culture

Character-oriented Cultural Practices and "Community of Preferences" as a New Fandom in Japan and Beyond

AKIKO SUGAWA-SHIMADA

What is "2.5-dimension (2.5 jigen)"?

In recent years, the term "2.5-dimension *(ni-ten-go jigen)*" has gained much attention within popular culture studies. The term "2.5 *jigen*" roughly means the space between the two-dimensional (fictional space where our imaginations and fantasy work) and the three-dimensional (reality where we physically exist). Within Japanese anime fandom, fans often use "two dimensions" to mean anime characters, stating, "I am only capable of loving the two-dimensional [characters] *(2 jigen shika aisenai)*." However, due to the growing success of cosplay and 2.5-D stage performances (theatrical adaptations of manga, anime, and videogames) since the early 2000s, the 2.5-D has begun to be used as an umbrella term to express virtuality embodied by actual human bodies as well as human bodies that look unreal, which I call "virtual corporality" *(kyokô teki shintai)*.

A magazine specializing in 2.5-D theatrical performances, *Stage Push!*, was published in 2014, and in 2016, the March issue of *Da Vinci*, Kadokawa's entertainment magazine featuring 2.5-D, was immediately sold out.[1] These magazines usually focus on 2.5-D stages under the name of "2.5 jigen." In 2018, when NHK's year-end traditional entertainment event, *Kôhaku utagassen* (Red and White Singing Festival) invited the singing group, Tôken danshi, from one of the most famous 2.5-D musicals, *Musical Tôken ranbu* as a guest, 2.5-D theatrical performances gained national recognition in Japan. Academic critical attention has been also drawn by some publications such as art and culture magazines *Yuriika* (2015, *Eureka*) and *Bijutsu techô* (2016 and 2016, *The Art Handbook*), featuring special issues on the 2.5-D cultural phenomenon. These magazines primarily focus on 2.5-D stages as cultural products.

The Japan 2.5 Dimensional Musical Association, founded in 2014, defines 2.5-dimensional musicals as "theatrical presentations based on Japanese manga, popular animation and video games."[2] This is the typical categorization of 2.5-D stages as seen from the production side for promotional purposes. However, fans use 2.5-D very differently, usually taking pleasure in realistic reproduction and reenactment of anime/manga/videogame characters ("virtual corporality"), fictional worlds, and the interaction between characters/actors and fans. As a matter of fact, 2.5-D theatrical performances are not stand-alone productions but, just like anime and manga, they have multiple episodes within a series, called a "season" (shiizun) in Japanese. For example, the first season of Musical Prince of Tennis ran from 2003 to 2010, with sixteen plays (or episodes) in which each had a run of between a few days and a few months.[3] The merchandise sold during the event is one of the major motivations for fans to visit theaters. They exchange their unwanted merchandise among fans outside the theaters for their desired products, such as canned badges and photos of cast members in costumes. This exercise is called "trading," and these venues serve as sites for fans to construct their communities of fandom. As such, if we can extend the scope from the cultural products themselves to the fans' engagement developed through their deep commitment to character-oriented consumption of popular culture, then 2.5-D can be utilized as a means to detect wider cultural phenomenon among fans of popular cultural contents such as manga, anime, and videogames.

I define the 2.5-dimensional culture as "cultural practices which reproduce the fictional space of contemporary popular cultural products (such as manga, anime, and videogames) along with the fans' interplay between the real and fictional spaces."[4] Emerging as a cultural phenomenon in Japan in the early 2000s, 2.5-dimensional culture includes 2.5-D theatrical performances, cosplay, voice-actor/character concerts such as Love Live! School Idol Project (2010–), anime-induced tourism (also known as contents tourism), cheering-along version of anime movie screening (ôenjôei), and virtual YouTuber (or V-Tubers, such as Kizuna Ai). Ôenjôei is a special screening at movie theaters where the audience is allowed to shout out and cheer for fictional characters in the movies while waving colorful light sticks. Some ôenjôei allow cosplay, which is usually inappropriate in regular screenings. Although the ôenjôei style has a long history in Japan, ôenjôei became widely known to people by the success of The King of Prism by Pretty Rhythm (2016). In other words, 2.5-D consists of any cultural practices exercised within the blurry boundary between the 2nd- and 3rd-dimensional spaces and with the deep participation of fans: all of these cultural phenomena emerged in the space between fictions (2-D) and reality (3-D) through their fans' commitment to these cultural products.

During the 1970–80s when the second anime boom broke out, the term "2.5" (the abbreviated version of 2.5-D) originally meant animations' voice actors *(seiyû)*. Regarding the functions of seiyû, Nozawa Shunsuke suggests:

> The metaphor of *naka no hito* [person inside] frames *seiyû* as mediators or mediums of the character-driven convergence culture. It conjures up an imagination on the verge, where reality and fantasy meet but never merge. As subcultural participants often say, *seiyû* are seen as inhabiting an interstitial dimension between "3D" reality and "2D" fantasy— "2.5D." *Seiyû* are mediums on the verge.[5]

Indeed, seiyû have an important function in linking fantasy to reality with the help of the corporality of the seiyû's bodies and voices. Yet, since the late 1990s in the digital era, fans' consumption and production of popular culture have drastically changed.

Regarding tourists of "contents tourism" (or anime-induced tourism), Okamoto Takeshi explains how fans enjoy consuming anime's content by migrating among three spaces: the fictional space of anime story and characters, the cyber space where they exchange the information about stories as well as the stages of the stories, and the physical spaces that are seen as "anime's sacred sites" for fans, places that are also where local people spend their life.[6] This model is applicable to 2.5-D culture. Fans as active consumers and producers randomly access these spaces and find many kinds of pleasure. In addition, reality and fantasy blur through the development of visual technology like virtual reality (VR) and augmented reality (AR) and users' communication by social media such as Twitter. These changes in visual technology and communication style affect our perception of "the real." It is 2.5-D theatrical performances that clearly exemplify the 2.5-D phenomena in terms of virtual corporality and fans' commitment to the 2.5-D space.

This article explores the major factors of the emergence of 2.5-D culture in Japan: character-oriented consumption induced by the full normalization of "media mix" (franchises in multiple media forms), the change of our perception of "reality," and fans' participation in 2.5-D culture. It then argues how 2.5-D theatrical performances serve as a means to address 2.5-D culture as fans' character-oriented consumption and production by focusing on examining the long-running 2.5-D theatrical performance series of *Musical Prince of Tennis* (2003–), and by analyzing Japanese and Chinese fans' method of consumption and use of 2.5-D theatrical performances. In their consumption practices, we see that fans of the 2.5-D theatrical performances create a new type of fandom, "communities of preferences," in which they are tied together as intimate strangers. In these kinds of fan communities, age, occupation, social status, marital status, nationality, and ethnicity are not the focus of attention and, as such, exhibit great potential for transnational communication.

Emerging 2.5-dimensional Culture in the Japanese Context: Character/World Consumption through Media Mix

Coined in the 1980s, "media mix" is the Japanese term meaning franchises of popular culture in multiple media forms. Oda Eiichiro's world-famous manga *One Piece* (1997–) typically exemplifies the media mix. It has been adapted into a TV anime (1999–), anime movies (2000–), novels (1999–), videogames (2000–), the Kabuki play, *Super Kabuki II One Piece* (2015–18), the entertainment shows, *One Piece Premier Show*, and *Sanji's Pirates Restaurant* in Universal Studio Japan (2011–), and *One Piece Live Attraction*, in Tokyo "One Piece" Tower (2015–).[7] Merchandise varies, ranging from stationary and T-shirts for children to jewelry and clothing for adults. Thus, regardless of media platforms, the variety of information oriented by characters and narrative worlds is generally called "contents" *(kontentsu)* in the Japanese media environment. Marc Steinberg defines the Japanese media mix as follows:

> [M]edia mix works as a system of objects and factors in media based on certain characters, narratives, and worlds *(sekai-kan)*. . . . Media mix is the feedback system between consumers and producers, which has developed to making consumers into producers.[8]

Steinberg argues that this system of franchises in multiple platforms is probably a counterpart of North American transmedia storytelling, but the continuum of narrative worlds is more flexible in the Japanese media mix. Ôtsuka Eiji argues that the origin of media-mix system (which he calls "narrative consumption")[9] was already observed in nineteenth-century Japan with *Sekai kômoku*, the guidebook to adapt *Taiheiki* (the fourteenth-century historical epic) into Kabuki, *Jôruri* (puppet theater) plays, and *kôdan* storytelling.[10] This sort of media-mix system was politically utilized during wartime with a comic-strip characters, *Yokusan ikka (The Yamatos).*[11] Drawing on

Ôtsuka's narrative consumption, Azuma Hiroki analyzes Japanese otaku culture by using his "database consumption theory": Japanese otaku take pleasure in consuming and using the database of the traits of characters of anime, manga, videogames, and other popular culture forms, which Azuma argues is a postmodern phenomenon. Ôtsuka, however, suggests that consumers' active commitment and use of character images (that is, the database) already functioned before the time of the modern period.[12] Although understandings of the historical timeline and continuum of the media mix are different between Ôtsuka and Azuma, they both do not deny that the characters and their narrative worlds are more focused on than the narrative per se.[13]

As such, one of the most important particularities of the consumption and production of anime is the ubiquity of anime characters. Indeed, the media-mix system, where stakeholders as well as fans use and create fictions based on database (the settings of characters and narrative worlds), was strategically introduced in anime from the advent of domestic TV anime in the 1960s. It is "a major turning point and inspiration for the development [of the Japanese media mix]."[14] However, it is also true that media-mix phenomenon has been accelerated and enhanced in accordance with the development of the internet and social media, which enable active participations of users/fans and easy access to other users/fans (which we will revisit later).

It is also important to note the local specifics of the media environment of Japanese TV programs for children and adults. As Steinberg suggests, the emergence of Japanese domestic TV anime serials in the 1960s served to disseminate today's media-mix system because they were majorly sponsored by toy and food companies whose products targeted children. Unlike in America, where advertisements of products aiming at children are strictly regulated, most of TV anime programs for children on the privately owned Japanese television networks inserted commercial films between each anime's episode. For example, a thirty-minute anime program consists of the opening credits, part A (the first part of one episode), advertisements, part B (the latter part of one episode), the ending roll, and more advertisements. In the advertisement sections, character-images are often used, so that TV anime for children itself function as advertisements for merchandising products. Since Japanese audiences are accustomed to such a media environment from childhood, where anime characters serve to seamlessly connect their fantasy to audiences' reality, fictional character images are transfused throughout their daily life, allowing them to "experience" the embodiment of the fictional.

The Development of Visual Technology and the Change of Communication Style of Fans

2.5-D cultural phenomena began to emerge and disseminate in accordance with the development of the internet, social media, and visual technology. For instance, home videogames using virtual reality (VR) technology, which is used to express realistic environment through visual presentation by stimulating our sensory perceptions, began to be sold for a reasonable price in 2016. Through products like PlayStation VR, players could easily experience close and realistic interaction with fictional VR characters in the pseudo-reality space of their own home. More recently, with the development of smart phones, augmented reality (AR) is often used for tourist information and entertainment through activating specific applications installed into your personal mobile media.

Due to the development of visual technology and a ubiquitous network society, Andriana de Sauza e Sylva suggests that continuous connection to the internet and other users by mobile devices creates hybrid reality.[15] Infiltration of a sense of hybrid reality may be enhanced by the emergence of social media sites such as Twitters and Line in Japan and abroad. Fictional images of anime, for instance, are widely spread because of the media mix-environment that utilizes social media. Many of the fictional characters of anime, manga, and videogames have their own official Twitter accounts primarily for promotional purposes of the stakeholders. Characters of *Uta no prinsusama* (*Princes of Songs*, hereafter *Utapuri*) is a typical example. *Utapuri* is one of the most popular mediamix contents in Japan, starting as a Play-Station portable game for young women in 2010. It was adapted into a TV anime (2011–16), character/seiyû concerts (2013–17), theatrical performances (2017–18), an anime movie (2019), and other media, including a spinoff. In its official Twitter account, each handsome male character has his own personal account through which the characters (supposedly) send their own messages to the public almost daily. Their fans can send their own replies to the account too. The characters sometimes upload real photos, which they (supposed to) take themselves. These actions serve to seamlessly connect fictional characters to fans (Figure 1).

In such an environment, we can see how 2.5-D becomes ported to forms of media. In 2.5-D theatrical performances, in particular, actors/actresses thoroughly copy the appearances and nature of anime/manga/videogame characters. Fans can easily imagine that they pop up from the 2-D fictional

Figure 1. Screen capture of the Twitter account of Tokiya Ichinose in *Utapuri*.

world into the 3-D real world due to their precise copying and reenactment. In addition to the reenactment of the fictional world, actors/actresses show performances that are not described in the original works but which fans expect to see. The actors/actresses also eagerly report on lessons and backstage activities through social media. It facilitates the construction of multiple layers of hybrid reality, where fans enjoy interactions with characters and actors who play roles of characters, referring to narratives of the work the play is based on, amateur authors' derivative works, narratives of other 2.5-D plays in which the actors of the 2.5-D plays perform, and so on.

2.5-D Theatrical Performances and the Deep Participation of Fans

Since the early 2010s, due to the development of Twitter, fans of *Musical Prince of Tennis* (hereafter *Tenimyu*) eagerly connect themselves to other fans in cyberspace with their anonymity maintained. In the hybrid reality era, because cyberspace and the physical space are seamlessly connected, *Tenimyu* fans migrate among the three spaces (the fictional, cyber, and physical spaces) to construct the *Tenimyu* world as the 2.5-D space. Though the media-mix environment and development of social and visual technologies play major roles in facilitating the construction of 2.5-D space via fan interactions, it is not the case that fans are incapable of distinguishing between fantasy and reality. More precisely, they have a pleasurable interplay with the ambiguous boundary between fantasy and reality within 2.5-D space. 2.5-D theatrical performances typify this 2.5-D cultural phenomenon, which focuses on the method of character consumption and use of contents.

The first successful theatrical adaptation of manga, anime, and videogames was *Rose of the Versailles* (1974) performed by Takarazuka Revue Company, the Japanese all-female theatrical troop founded in 1914. Based on Ikeda Riyoko's shôjo manga of the same title on the French Revolution, Takarazuka actresses copied fictional characters with gaudy-colored make-up and flamboyant costumes. In the 1990s and 2000s, when the media-mix strategy was actively utilized in anime, the precise reproduction of fictional characters and reenactment of the narrative worlds in anime, manga, and videogames were emphasized in the concerts and plays of *Sakura Wars* (1997-2018) and *Musical Hunter x Hunter* (2000-2004). Both were performed by the seiyû who played the same character on stage as they did in the anime they dubbed. After these works, the number of the titles of anime's theatrical adaptation rose suddenly in 2008 and, with a large leap in 2012 with approximately 1000 titles produced.[16]

In distinction from the 2.5-D-like plays mentioned above, the success of *Tenimyu* led to constructing 2.5-D theatrical performances as a genre. *Tenimyu* is based on Konomi Takeshi's shônen manga *Prince of Tennis* (1999-2008), which was adapted into TV anime (2001-5), novels (2002-), anime movies (2005), and a live action movie (2006). *Prince of Tennis* is about boy tennis players from the junior high school Seishun Academy, in Tokyo, focusing on Echizen Ryoma, a thirteen-year-old returnee from America and the current world junior tennis champion. The story follows Ryoma's entrance to Seishun Academy's tennis club to the championship of the national junior high school tennis tournament. His teammates and opponents of other junior high school tennis clubs are all talented tennis players and have unique characteristics. Almost all the characters are handsome boys, which inspire female fans to produce numerous derivative works *(dôjinshi)* such as those of the Boys'

Love genre. Responding to such fan expectations, director, Ueshima Yukio intended to exclude female characters from *Tenimyu* although there are some important female characters in Konomi's manga, allowing female audiences/fans to enjoy seeing only attractive male bodies on the stage.[17]

The first season of *Tenimyu* began in 2003 and was an instant success. Due to the tight budget, casts for *Tenimyu* were auditioned and selected by their personal aura and how close the "spirit" of the candidates was to those of the anime character rather than the actors' popularity and fame. This is called the "Tenimyu method," one of the secrets of the great success of 2.5-D theatrical performances. In other words, characters' visuals are impressively foregrounded rather than the actors themselves, allowing fans to be absorbed into the 2.5-D space without being bothered by actors' images and private lives. Since the selected casts are young, almost unknown but promising actors, audiences/fans of the manga/anime versions of *Prince of Tennis* could primarily concentrate on the visual reproduction enabled by the precise copy of the fictional characters. Some fans arguably posted a message on the internet that "[the casts of *Tenimyu*] seemed to pop up from the 2-D fictional world. They are just 2.5-D."[18] This perception has gradually spread among fans to become the term 2.5-D to indicate some hybrid entity with fictionality of anime, manga, videogames, and reality.

Tenimyu is successful not only reproduction and reenactment but also in engaging in audiences/fans' expectations and getting them involved by coming down from the stage to audiences *(kyakuseki ori)*, seeing the audiences off to the corridor near the exit after the play *(o-miokuri)*, and the announcements and voice skits of characters before and after the performances *(kage nare)*. At the end of the play, there is a curtain call. During curtain call, audiences also sing songs together with the casts, waving lighting sticks. The casts do kyakuseki ori and give a high-five to audience members, making audiences feel as if the fictional characters may even physically touch them. As such, it is not just the actors but also the participation of audiences/fans that enables the 2.5-D space to be constructed, because, as Erika Fischer-Lichte suggests, "[a] performance is inseparable from the bodily co-presence of various groups of people who come together as actors and spectators."[19] Here we see this enacted in a very literal form.

Besides the musical whose stories (episodes) are adapted from Konomi's manga and its anime adaptation, the *Tenimyu* world extends to single annual concerts and events: *Dream Live* (the concert by several casts of *Tenimyu*), *Team Live* (the concert by the casts of other school tennis teams), and *Culture*

Festival and *Sports Festival* (the events performed by the casts that copy festivals in Japanese schools). In addition, the author Konomi occasionally has his own concert where he is joined by the *Tenimyu* casts playing the characters of *Prince of Tennis*, forming a 2.5-D space where the author of the manga interacts with his manga characters (via the casts' bodies) and fans/audiences. Such character-oriented media mix serves to induce fans' character consumption and active commitment to the 2.5-D space.

Fans' derivative works on *Tenimyu* also aid in constructing the 2.5-D space. In the late 2000s, *Tenimyu* fans made short video clips called *soramimi* (mishearing) by using scenes from the DVDs of *Tenimyu*, sharing them on YouTube and *Niconico Dôga* (hereafter Niconico). In the soramimi video, some subtitles are inserted to create different meanings by using misheard words, making fun of the poor enunciation of the young cast members. For instance, "*Haiagare, Kaidô!*" (Get up from the bottom rung, Kaidô!) is misheard for "*Hariyagare, kairo!*" (Just put on a heating pad!) as a play on words. Flowing across the screen of the Niconico video, are the amusing comments of other users, fostering further online interactions. These soramimi videos helped to trigger the *Tenimyu* boom because they induced many fans who enjoyed the parodies to go to the theater to see "the real performances."

Such soramimi videos gradually decreased as the quality of the actors' performance increased. A growing number of fans of *Tenimyu* began "trading" merchandizing products (photos, budges, stickers, etc.) near the theater entrances, exchanging unwanted ones for those they wanted. As one of the characteristics of 2.5-D plays, some merchandizing products such as badges and photos are sold as a set of different characters, called *randamu guzzu* (random goods). Fans select their favorite ones from the set and trade out the unwanted ones. Thus, this style of merchandizing can facilitate fans' trading.

As mentioned above, participation of fans is vital to create the 2.5-D space. Fans show their affection for the characters/actors they love by purchasing all the goods related to them. This practice is called *ofuse* ("donation to gods") and to gift the goods or rent DVDs to their friends who are unfamiliar with the 2.5-D theatrical performances is called *fukyô* ("missionary work"), as it is expanding their network. This was originally practiced in a spontaneous manner among fans; however, current stakeholders deftly utilize these fan practices as a strategy for the media mix. As Ôtsuka suggests, such material practices under the guise of the spiritual or religious terms are, on one hand, fans' initiatives but, on the other hand, they can be taken as pitfalls of the media mix because the fans may be unaware of being manipulated.[20]

International Fans of 2.5-D Theatrical Performances and Communities of Preferences

As Japanese anime has been disseminated throughout the world, 2.5-D theatrical performances, especially those adapted from well-known anime/
manga, have been an instant success overseas, especially in Asia. *Tenimyu*
made the first Asia tour to Taiwan and South Korea in 2008. Since its success,
the number of the 2.5-D theatrical performances have been exported to Asian
countries: *Musical Kuro shitsuji (Black Butler)* to China from 2015, *Live Spectacle NARUTO* to China, Singapore, and Macao in 2015, followed by Malaysia
in 2016, and the videogame-based *Musical Tôken ranbu (Boisterous Dances of
Swords)* to China in 2017. *Musical Tôken ranbu* also had a tour in Paris in 2018,
the first 2.5-D staged in Europe, but here I will focus mainly on China.

With the increase of overseas performances of the 2.5-D plays, the number
of overseas fans also drastically increased. In this section I examine Chinese
fans of 2.5-D theatrical performances and analyze how they use Japanese
2.5-D plays to construct their fandom. I conducted a focus group interview
with six Chinese female fans who live in Tokyo in April 2018 and individual
interviews with four Chinese fans in Shanghai in 2016 and 2018. In the focus
group, two are Chinese fans I met at the theater, who then invited other participants. For the individual interviews, one was with a young Chinese woman
I met at the theater, and others were with women who were invited by others.
The participants were all in their twenties and loved Japanese popular culture
such as manga, anime, and music as a child.

Before going into the details of the Chinese fans, I would like to discuss
the type of communities that we see in Japan. As Kitada Akihiro notes, compared to hobbies like fashion, music, and novels, anime is a more effective
one for making friends with other anime fans, since anime fans often feel an
inferiority complex with regard to other respectable hobbies.[21] This is also
gendered. Regarding the relationship between manga readership and gender,
Dan Yasuaki suggests that female regular manga readers tend to make more
personal networks with other female readers by using their favorite manga
than male regular manga readers do.[22] Along similar lines, I would also argue
that female 2.5-D play fans construct communities among fans through sharing the same or similar preferences, which I call "communities of preferences."
In the communities of preferences, while maintaining their anonymity and
distance, fans are weakly tied by sharing their preferences in a community,
but they have the freedom to hop to other communities. As mentioned in the

previous section, Japanese female fans of 2.5-D theatrical performances interact with other fans through Twitter and near the theater entrances. Through the trading, they often make friends and go to other 2.5-D plays together. Since anonymity is kept, those fans demographically vary in age, marital status, business career, and social class. As Tomita Hidenori suggests, they are "intimate strangers,"[23] being weakly tied but unfamiliar to their backgrounds. Although similar communities of preferences have been observed in other hobbies such as rock 'n roll, novels, sports, and so on, the communities of preferences related to 2.5-D culture are distinguishable in that 2.5-D fans tend to hide their preferences of anime, manga, and game-related hobbies. For instance, some people feel ashamed and have never told of their enthusiasm toward 2.5-D theatrical performances to their colleagues, classmates, and even family members. Therefore, when they find someone with similar or same preferences, they would immediately feel intimacy toward them.

Similarly, through the 2.5-D theatrical performances, four Chinese fans of the focus group met through Weibo (Chinese Twitter-like social media) except the two who were already friends from their university in China. They also have experiences of making friends with some Japanese fans through trading the merchandize. One of the interviewees stated that, "If I found someone who seems to be a fan of the characters/casts I love, I immediately feel an intimacy with her. I don't care where we are from. We can be connected by the same preference." Other interviewees in the group agreed with her, saying that "Japanese fans are happy to find us being fond of Japanese 2.5-D plays." This can testify that the communities of preferences also function for non-Japanese 2.5-D play fans.

A Chinese fan in Shanghai made a similar remark. She frequently comes to Japan over the weekends to see 2.5-D theatrical performances where her favorite actor plays. She met Japanese fans of the male actor through his events and trading of the merchandise such as his photos. Another interviewee collected information through the Japanese Facebook page of her favorite actor/character of *Live Spectacle NARUTO* by using a special application to access it from China. She has never been to Japan, but she interacted with some Japanese fans by exchanging the information on the actor/character online. She said, "They probably don't know I'm Chinese because I use a Japanese username to communicate with them in Japanese. But again, I wonder if they might know because my Japanese is not accurate."

These samples of the interviews are so limited that it cannot be fully proved that all Chinese 2.5-D play fans successfully construct communities of preferences. However, it should be noted that, at least for the participants, the ways of constructing communities of preferences through 2.5-D theatrical performances are strikingly similar for both Japanese and Chinese fans. This displays quite a lot of potential for transnational and even transethnic understanding. This is also not isolated to Asia. As mentioned above, 2.5 D plays were also performed and probably will be performed more in Europe. Some French fans of *Musical Tôken ranbu*, for instance, have created a large community through social media, attempting to connect other fans who are far from Paris. The fans in France are demographically diverse, and have stated that they realized that they would have never met otherwise.[24] In sum, communities of preference are not necessarily limited to national or regional boundaries.

Conclusion

The 2.5-D culture emerged due to the dissemination of the media mix, the development of visual presentations such as VR and AR that affected our perception of reality, and the development of social media and mobile media devices that enabled continuous connection to other users and interactive communications with them. These factors constructed a hybrid reality where we take pleasure in blurring the boundary between fantasy and reality. In such a media environment, the binary opposition between producers and consumers blurs because fans' participation in the contents is very important to construct the 2.5-D space. Fans' derivative works (fanfictions, dôjinshi, fanart, fanvideos, and even fangames) are also influential to other fans and even stakeholders in that if the producers/actors ignore fans' expectations, the 2.5-D space may be immediately destroyed.

By utilizing "virtual corporality," 2.5-D theatrical performances fulfill the fans' desire for physically experiencing the presence of fictional characters in reality. Moreover, ways of female fans' consumption and using of 2.5-D plays are complex: they take pleasure in interpreting the relationships between fictional characters in the story, cross-referring to the relationships of actors with other characters in their real life.[25] Although they are rivals in the story, some actors who play the rival characters are very close in reality. To find the gap, some fans are thrilled when they imagine that the rival characters get along well when they are out-of-stage. Such cross-referential readings of fans' imagination are shared in these communities of preferences, which are also constructed through trading of merchandizing products of 2.5-D theatrical performances that lead to further interactions and cross-referring. This way of extending personal networks has much potential for mutual communication regardless of age, marital status, academic history, social position, and even ethnicity and nationality.

Akiko Sugawa-Shimada, PhD, is a professor in the Graduate School of Urban Innovation at Yokohama National University, Japan. Dr. Sugawa-Shimada is the author of a number of books and articles on anime, manga, and cultural studies, including *Girls and Magic: How Have Girl Heroes Been Accepted?* (2013, won the 2014 Japan Society of Animation Studies Award, in Japanese), chapters in the books *Japanese Animation: East Asian Perspectives* (2013), *Teaching Japanese Popular Culture* (2016), *Shojo Across Media* (2019), and *Women's Manga in Asia and Beyond* (2019), and a co-author of *Contents Tourism in Japan* (2017). Her website is akikosugawa.2-d.jp.

This work was supported by JSPS KAKENHI Grant Number 17K18459.

Notes

1. *"2.5 jigen tokushuu no Da Vinci 3gatsu go mikka de amazon urikire!"* ("The March issue of *Da Vinci* featuring 2.5-D sold out three days after the publication in amazon store."), *Da Vinci News*, February 9, 2016. https://ddnavi.com/news /285018/a/ (accessed June 1, 2018).
2. Japan 2.5 Dimensional Musical Association, Pamphlet, https://www.j25musical .jp/user/img/download/J2.5D_pamphet.pdf, 3.
3. *Musical Prince of Tennis*, "Koremade no kôen (List of plays)," https//www.tennimu .com/archive, accessed on January 4, 2019.
4. Sugawa Akiko, "Fantajii ni asobu: Pafômansu toshiteno 2.5jigen bunka ryôiki to imajineshon (Interplay with fantasy: The 2.5-D cultural space and our imagination)," *Yuriika (Eureka)*, Special Issue: 2.5-jigen (2.5-Dimension), (2015: 41–47).
5. Nozawa Shunsuke, "Ensoulment and Effacement in Japanese Voice Acting," *Media Convergence in Japan,* ed. Patrick W. Galbraith and Jason G. Karlin (Minnesota: Kinema Club, 2016: 169-199), 170.
6. Okamoto Takeshi. "Kontentsu tuurizumu no kuukan (Spaces of contents tourism)," *Kontentsu tuurizumu kenkyu: Jôhô shakai no kankô koudou to chiiki shinkou* (A study on contents tourism: tourism actions and regional development), (Tokyo: Fukumura shuppan, 2015,: 50–51), 51.

7. Sugawa Akiko, "*Butai, têma paaku ni okeru Wan Piisu sekaikan no kôchiku* (Constructions of the narrative worlds of *One Piece* in theaters and theme parks)," *Media Contents Studies*, ed. Takeshi Okamoto (Tokyo: Nakanishiya shuppan, 2020), 119–30.

8. Marc Steinberg, *Nihon wa naze "media mix suru kuni" nanoka* (Tokyo: Kadokawa, 2015), 35. From the Japanese translation, and thus, it is my translation.

9. Ôtsuka Eiji, *Teihon Monogatari shôhi ron (The theory of narrative consumption, authentic text)* (Tokyo: Kadokawa, 2001).

10. Ôtsuka Eiji, *Monogatari shôhi ron kai (The theory of narrative consumption)*, revised version, (Tokyo: Ascii shinsho, 2012), 46–48.

11. Ôtsuka Eiji, "*Senjika no media mikkusu: Yokusan ikka to tonarigumi* (Wartime media mix: Yokusan family and neighborhood associations)," in *Media mix mobilization (Dôin no media mikkusu: "sôsaku suru taishuu" no senjika, sengo)* (Tokyo: Shibunkaku shuppan, 2017): 29–53, 32–33.

12. Ôtsuka, *Media Mix mobilization*, 30.

13. Azuma Hiroki, *Otaku: Japan's Database Animals*, trans. Jonathan E. Abel and Shinon Kono (Minneapolis and London: University of Minnesota Press, 2009), 31, 48.

14. Marc Steinberg, *Media Mix: Franchising Toys and Characters in Japan* (Minneapolis: University of Minnesota Press, 2012), viii.

15. Adriana de Sauza e Sylva, "From cyber to hybrid: mobile technology as interfaces of hybrid reality" (*Space and Culture* 9, (2006):261–78), 261.

16. Pia, *Zennen hi 21% zo, Kyuu seichô no 2.5-jigen myuujikaru shijô/pia sôken ga chôsa kekka wo kôhyô, Pia* (August 1, 2018) n.p. https://corporate.pia.jp/news/detail_live_enta20180801_25.html. (Accessed December 20, 2018).

17. Ueshima Yukio, "*Hikari to dansu de manga wo butai ni henkan suru* (Manga is adapted into a play with lights and dances)," *The Art Handbook*, Special Issue 2.5-jigen bunka (July 2016: 26–31), 26.

18. Sugawa Akiko, "*Fantajii ni asobu: pafômansu toshiteno 2.5jigen bunka ryôiki to imajineshon* (Interplay with fantasy: The 2.5-D cultural space and our imagination)," *Yuriika (Eureka)*, Special Issue: 2.5-jigen (2.5-Dimension), (2015: 41–47), 42.

19. Erika Fischer-Lichte, *The Routledge Introduction to Theatre and Performance Studies* (London: Routledge, 2014), 18.

20. Ôtsuka, *Media Mix Mobilization*, 30.

21. Kitada Akihiro, "*Dôbutsutachi no rakuen to môsô no kyodôtai: otaku bunka juyô yôshiki to jendaa*" (Animals' paradise and communities of imagination: An acceptance style of otaku culture and gender), eds., *Shakai ni totte shumi towa nanika: Bunka shakaigaku no houhou kijun (What is hobby for society?: Methodological standards in cultural sociology)*, ed. Akihiro Kitada and Kaitaiken (Tokyo: Kawade Books, 2017: 261–314), 264.

22. Dan Yasuaki, "*Manga dokusho keiken to jendaa: Futatsu no chôsa no bunseki kara* (Manga readership and gender: Two research and analyses)," *Shakai ni totte shumi towa nanika: Bunka shakaigaku no houhou kijun (What is hobby for society?:*

Methodological standards in cultural sociology), ed. Akihiro Kitada and Kaitaiken (Tokyo: Kawade Books, 2017:179–201), 197.

23. Tomita Hidenori. *Intimate Stranger: Tokumeisei to kôkyosei wo meguru bunka shakaiteki kenkyuu (Intimate strangers: A socio-cultural study on anonymity and commonality)* (Osaka: Kansai daigaku shuppan, 2017).

24. Nihon Hôsô Kyokai (NHK broadcasting network), "Shibuya note presents: *Musical Token ranbu, 2.5jigen kara sekai e* (Shibuya note presents: Musical Token love from 2.5-D to the world)," aired on 27 October 2019.

25. Azuma Sonoko, *Takarazuka, yaoi, ai no yomikae: Popyura karuchaa to josei no shakaigaku (Takarazuka, yaoi, interpretation of love: Sociology of popular culture and women)* (Tokyo: Shinyosha, 2015).

Pedestrian Media Mix

The Birth of Otaku Sanctuaries in Tokyo

EDMOND ERNEST DIT ALBAN

> Could you ask Otome-Games publishers why they don't want us to do Cosplay anymore? I don't get why we are 'tarnishing the character's image just by dressing like them anyways. You know, one of my friends doing a fanzine and amateur (dôjin) item was asked to stop selling it online last month. It's like they are scared of us taking over their right to use the characters? But we still buy official merch(andise), you know?
>
> —K-ko, 26, personal interview, July 2015

When interviewing a group of women performing dances and cosplay in Otome Road (Ikebukuro, Tokyo) in July 2015, it became clear to me that their main concerns went directly to the question of how the "recycling practices" fundamental to their communities were becoming more regulated by publishing companies *(enujîriyô)*, specifically at convention sites and so-called otaku sanctuaries *(otaku no seichi)*. They also mentioned how trading randomized lottery, crane-games, or capsule toy prices tended to be forbidden by official distribution sites; posters around the local Animate retail store prohibited "salvage exchanges of randomly distributed merchandise," describing this behavior as "cheating." Because parts of the local female fan communities felt a certain urgency to address the gradual policing of how they recycle media and content, it is important to reconstruct their role in the history of the territories important to otaku culture as well as its industries.

Consequently, when describing otaku sanctuaries, I find it relevant to advocate for the recognition of "recycling" practices as one of their markers.[1] For instance, most urban sanctuaries are constructed around "recycle shops": secondhand stores where otaku sell and purchase used media. In addition, "recycling" also occurs in fanzines, cosplay, and other fan practices that reuse the content from favorite shows to produce amateur media and invent new performances in a manner similar to remix cultures. By examining these "recycling" practices, this article explores the entangled histories of otaku sanctuaries and anime business models to reveal how female consumers acted both in the production of new social spaces as well as in new media production models. Adopting a spatial approach—that is to say, one looking at the urban space occupied by otaku cultures—I analyze the conjoined transformations of otaku sanctuaries and so-called media-mix strategies from the material convergence of large scale recycling practices convalescing in Otome Road's various networks of bookstores, anime paraphernalia distributors, fans conventions, and pedestrian consumers transporting media across cities.[2]

The urban networks and (female) pedestrian actors supporting the already visible parts of otaku history are terribly understudied. Recognizing an alternative otaku history centered on the recycling spaces at the heart of otaku sanctuaries may nuance official (as well as academic) discourses that heavily focus on industrial practices. When looking at Otome Road's birth, the conjoined evolution of recycling shops with media-mix tendencies narrate the dialectics between a large spectrum of both amateur and industrial projects of space, using, despite their differences, similar places, practices, and techniques: from fans to publishers and distributors, the otaku cultural movement reuses images to build new media spreading across an urban milieu.[3] Therefore, in light of Thomas Lamarre's notion of *anime ecology*,[4] I propose to connect the already well-known production models of "reuse" in manga, anime, and video games in Japan with the pedestrian recycling practices of otaku sanctuaries: the remixing, reusing, or reappropriating of "used" images and media can also be seen as sustaining the production of new merchandise and spaces of circulation. Moreover, the repeated transit of multiple female and male otaku communities through Japanese cities invites a more comprehensive overview of how otaku subcultures occupy space and negotiate their place in society by producing or invading the leisure industry's territories.[5]

Otome Road's case in Ikebukuro, in particular, demonstrates how sanctuaries mediate the frequently controversial relations of fans to publishers. Since the early 1980s its geographies have represented the collaboration and confrontation of pedestrian communities struggling to find their own space, with publishers reusing fan's energy to refine media-mix models. Responding to the underestimation of the sociopolitical stakes of recycling tendencies in the study of otaku history, space, and politics, I would like to contribute to previous analyses of otaku spaces in Tokyo that originally mapped the urban inscription of otaku consumption by focusing on recycling, an "obvious" yet understudied aspect of the constitution of this fan mecca. The current growth of sanctuaries' territories around secondhand shops furthermore highlights how pedestrian recycling practices mediate the otaku cultural industry's relation to urban space.[6] In this way, my method approaches the evolution of the geographies of anime and manga paraphernalia circulation in Ikebukuro over the last few decades through the transformation of industrial media-mix practices and strategies.

As such, this work combines ethnographic materials from interviews with industry representatives and fans with the mapping of media and locations of anime, manga, and video game circulation that led to the emergence of Otome Road. Because of the scale of otaku sanctuaries' history in Ikebukuro, I will mostly focus on transitions occurring between the late 1980s and early 2000s. This article only covers the spatial dialogue between the industrial models of multimedia, world-consumption and character-media mix with the progressive stabilization of otaku spaces in Ikebukuro.[7] I conclude that most of the local figures of the otaku industry, such as paraphernalia distributor Animate or publisher Kadokawa, worked as "ethnographers" who followed the urban circulation of commodities and consumers in these sanctuaries. These institutions started to grasp the urban dimension of otaku subcultures from local manga bookstores and other small shops responding to pedestrian consumers' demand evinced by their amateurish take on media production. The frequent disputes opposing fans and now-established industrials could subsequently result from their common set of practices spatially and materially born within the recycling practices occurring in otaku sanctuaries.

A Short Introduction to the Study of Otaku Sanctuaries: Institutions, Objects, Geographies

Since the late 1990s the presence of anime, manga and video game "otaku" subcultures has become more and more present in cities across Japan.[8] Fan Meccas, also known as otaku sanctuaries, have subsequently grown in many regions across the country. Although most definitions of sanctuaries tend to focus on rural areas like Shirakawagô, the closest locations of otaku culture within the landscape of everyday life for many in Japan nevertheless remain in urban areas like Akihabara, Nakano, and Ikebukuro in Tokyo, or Nihonbashi in Osaka. What, then, is an urban otaku sanctuary?[9]

Otaku sanctuaries situated in Japanese cities are often built around an agglomeration of secondhand shops (*risaikuru shoppu*). As an example, in Ikebukuro, the historical heart of "the maidens' road" sanctuary (Otome Road) assembles various otaku niche markets targeting female audiences: recycle shops sell manga and novel slash fictions, women's video games, anime DVDs and CDs, musical or theater goods, and merchandise representing fictional attractive male characters from various series. Otome Road's territories have expanded from the secondhand locations near the local Sunshine City Mall to multiple official retail stores closer to the Ikebukuro Japan Railway station. Nowadays, the routes leading from the East to the West embody the circulation of images, media, and pedestrians between new and used economies. For instance, after otaku media is purchased in the anime paraphernalia supermarket Animate, fanzine retail store Toranoana, or women's games distributor Stella Worth, most of it ends up in secondhand shops. In this manner, Otome Road's territories are centered on local secondhand economies formed by the pedestrian circulation of otaku media, transported by women. Local networks emerged as toys, accessories, books, and other merchandise traveled from retail stores and fanzine conventions to secondhand shops.

Recent changes since the 2010s include the growth of collaboration cafés that join collectible merchandise with colorful food and drinks inspired by anime characters. Another noticeable element is the multiplication of trading spots in nearby parks. These spaces accentuate a decrease in the fanzine scene and space in secondhand shops now invaded by official media produced monthly by cafés and industry distributors alike. These developments are responded to in turn by the pedestrian consumers. For example, while the current focus on video games and monthly events in media-mix strategies materializes a certain industrial "project of space" that forces pedestrian consumers to move across specific locations, fans also invent new places to meet, mostly in parks (Figure 1), where they recycle images outside of official routes.[10] As such, transporting, exchanging, and recycling media and content in sanctuaries positions otaku pedestrians between institutions and moments of their capture. The motion of pedestrians itself amplifies and at times contradicts media-mix strategies. For these reasons, I propose to explain the evolution of media-mix models in light of the transformations of the routes of fan circulation in Otome Road: the boom of "reuse" strategies in the 1990s and 2000s otaku industry was in fact inspired by the discovery of otaku sanctuaries' local recycling ecologies.[11]

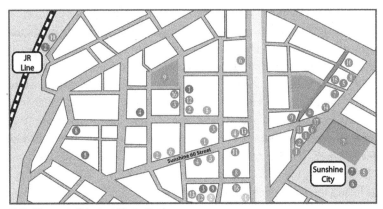

2018 : The current dialectics of Otome-Road

Official and New Media Retail Circuits :
① **Animate** : The "anime supermarket" changed location again in 2012, this time at the heart of East Ikebukuro.
② **P Parco** : This department store often proposes to Drama CD brands like Rejet to sell their merchandise in short-time events.
③ **Stella Worth** : "Stella" is the biggest Otome-Game and Drama CDs retail store in the sanctuary (2011).
④ **Tora no Ana** : Manga bookstore (Opened in 2012, changed into a all women's fanzine store in 2017).
⑤ **Tora no Ana** : Manga bookstore (Opened in 2013, former women's fanzine store).
⑥ **J World** : Shûeisha's official Shônen Jump store.
⑦ **Pokémon Center** : (*2014*).
⑧ **Meikidô** : Books and fanzine (2015).
⑨ **Gamers** : Manga bookstore (Changed location in the late 2000s)

Leisure spots :
① **Sega Gigo**: Arcade (Game Center) (1993).
② **Adores** : Arcade (Game Center).
③ **Project Adores** : Arcade (Game Center) (2012).
④ **St Tropez** : Arcade (Game Center).
⑤ **Karaoke no Tetsujin** : A karaoke featuring monthly collaborations with Otome-Games.
⑥ **Sunshine Cinema** (*1985*)

Recycle shops and used Media :
① **Lashinbang** : Used "character goods".
② **Lashinbang Multimedia** : Games CDs and DVDs.
③ **Lashinbang** : Used "character goods" (Opened in the basement in 2013 and extended to the full building in 2015).
④ **K-Books Select** : A recycle shop with shifting themes: idols, sportsmen and historical characters from anime and manga series.
⑤ **K-Books Fanzine** : Old and new (until 2018) women fanzine.
⑥ **K-Books Anime** : Renamed "Otome no Mori", first floor focuses on Otome-Games and second on sport manga and anime paraphernalia.
⑦ **K-Books Live** : Former K-Books multimedia and used books, shifted from slash romances media to Otome-Game boy's bands. (2018)
⑧ **K-Books Cast/Voice** : Musical related goods.

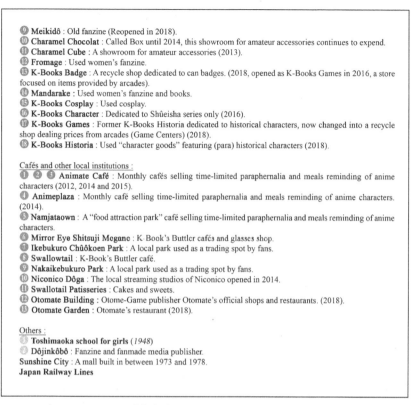

⑨ **Meikidô** : Old fanzine (Reopened in 2018).
⑩ **Charamel Chocolat** : Called Box until 2014, this showroom for amateur accessories continues to expend.
⑪ **Charamel Cube** : A showroom for amateur accessories (2013).
⑫ **Fromage** : Used women's fanzine.
⑬ **K-Books Badge** : A recycle shop dedicated to can badges. (2018, opened as K-Books Games in 2016, a store focused on items provided by arcades).
⑭ **Mandarake** : Used women's fanzine and books.
⑮ **K-Books Cosplay** : Used cosplay.
⑯ **K-Books Character** : Dedicated to Shûeisha series only (2016).
⑰ **K-Books Games** : Former K-Books Historia dedicated to historical characters, now changed into a recycle shop dealing prices from arcades (Game Centers) (2018).
⑱ **K-Books Historia** : Used "character goods" featuring (para) historical characters (2018).

Cafés and other local institutions :
① ② ③ **Animate Café** : Monthly cafés selling time-limited paraphernalia and meals reminding of anime characters (2012, 2014 and 2015).
④ **Animeplaza** : Monthly café selling time-limited paraphernalia and meals reminding of anime characters. (2014).
⑤ **Namjataown** : A "food attraction park" café selling time-limited paraphernalia and meals reminding of anime characters.
⑥ **Mirror Eye Shitsuji Megane** : K-Book's Buttler cafés and glasses shop.
⑦ **Ikebukuro Chûôkoen Park** : A local park used as a trading spot by fans.
⑧ **Swallowtail** : K-Book's Buttler café.
⑨ **Nakaikebukuro Park** : A local park used as a trading spot by fans.
⑩ **Niconico Dôga** : The local streaming studios of Niconico opened in 2014.
⑪ **Swallotail Patisseries** : Cakes and sweets.
⑫ **Otomate Building** : Otome-Game publisher Otomate's official shops and restaurants. (2018).
⑬ **Otomate Garden** : Otomate's restaurant (2018).

Others :
① **Toshimaoka school for girls** (*1948*)
② **Dôjinkôbô** : Fanzine and fanmade media publisher.
Sunshine City : A mall built in between 1973 and 1978.
Japan Railway Lines

Figure 1. The current state of Ikebukuro in 2018. Map produced by Edmond Ernest dit Alban during a fieldwork in June 2018. The progressive disappearance of books and fanzines from recycle shops indicates a recent shift in the local recycling economies leaning toward anime goods and events.

1980s–1990s: MULTIMEDIA BOOKSTORES AND THE
URBAN CONVERGENCE RECYCLING PRACTICES

It was just after I went to my first Yaoi convention in the Sunshine City.
I stopped at a bookstore named Animate before catching my train.
There was a tiny Captain Tsubasa pen case and I spent all the money my
mother gave me for my birthday on school supplies. Well, you know, the
few coins I had left after buying too many fanzines. (Laughs).

—Bko, 43, former student at the Toshimaoka School
for girls (Ikebukuro), personal interview, August 2015

The scant research that focuses on Ikebukuro and Otome Road tends to focus
on the more recent transformations of the area: there is a short report by
Morikawa Ka'ichirô published in 2005 mapping the main infrastructures of
the sanctuary and another by Sugiura Yumiko describing its emergence in
2006.[12] Because of this dearth of existing research for earlier eras, recovering
the earlier roots of Otome Road needs to cross-reference various other sources
including consumer and shop staff interviews as well as newspaper articles.[13]
Subsequently, when mapping the first introduction of anime and manga shops
in the neighborhood in the early 1980s, it was difficult to find the present logics
of sanctuaries relying on the circulation of content, media and people trans-
forming the "new" into the "used." In addition, since the 2000s, the growth of
secondhand shops focused on accessories such as towels, badges key-holders,
clear files, and other items based on popular male characters, products that did
not even exist in the early days of manga bookstores. In consideration of this, it
is important to note that the evolution of media-mix products is subsequently
underdocumented and often disappears with the items themselves.

With these conditions in mind, in this section I want to describe how in
the late 1980s the recently emerged bookstore ecology of Ikebukuro helped
to shape new media-mix strategies while responding to the local needs of
pedestrian communities. Because these institutions recycled official prepro-
duction materials and celluloid sheets used during the creation of manga and
anime, manga bookstores sustained a certain circulation of character images
between studios, shops, and fanzine conventions. As such, I would suggest
that women's otaku fanzine culture was heavily influenced by the first generations of these "character goods" representing the actual process of media
production. In addition, bookstore merchandise such as posters, postcards,
and magazines were recycled from the "trash" of official materials and then

reused by fans to produce their own media. Otaku discourses in the 1990s tended to focus on VHS tapes as the main media sustaining the otaku movement, and VHS would have made certain styles of animation accessible and recognizable.[14] Looking at the women's community and their consumption of character goods, however, points at other material objects in the late 1970s and 1980s that contributed to the emergence of semi-amateur practices and theorization of manga and anime.

Such material objects include postcards, magazines, and, later, illustration books (setteishū), which all gave fans models to copy from. In addition to that, bookstores also sold the basic tools to produce fanzines: drawing and school supplies. As most scholars working on female fanzines have also noticed, the main audiences of these products in the mid-1980s were schoolgirls. Considering the circulation of women in Ikebukuro at the time, and their increasing involvement in fanzine culture, it is plausible that the convergence of local fanzine conventions with bookstores had supported fanzine creations. The growth of conventions in the mid-1980s might be explained by the stabilization of the bookstore merchandise ecology in the routes of the pedestrian consumers of Ikebukuro's "Girlscape," a space invented by certain department stores to promote feminine mobility and consumption.[15] Early sanctuaries therefore formed a specific media ecology in which the labor of local stores met fan labor. In what follows, I will demonstrate how the transformation of media-mix strategies in the late 1980s started within the perimeter of bookstores as the transformation of images into new media commodities met an emergent secondhand economy increasingly including fanzine and fan made media into industrial strategies.

To better explore this, I would like to apply the conceptions of manga and anime's techniques of moving images already inherent in the media, and move it toward examining how these techniques induced the recycling of content and media in broad terms. Scholars such as Thomas Lamarre, Ian Condry, and Marc Steinberg have already stressed the importance of the celluloid bank— where images are stored for reuse in later sequences—in the making of anime and its paraphernalia.[16] Building on this, I suggest that otaku sanctuaries highlight the material and spatial dispersion of recycled images in cities as well as the invention of location-specific merchandise limited in time, space, and numbers for niche markets. In other words, media-mix practices reusing the character images to produce new commodities also transformed alongside the emergence of certain urban territories of commodity and consumer circulation; the early sanctuary in Ikebukuro reunited various types of recycled images transported by pedestrians, exposed alongside media complexes at home and re-appropriated in fan conventions.[17]

Thus, Ikebukuro's local networks described by the circulation of image-based commodities enabled the convergence of "official" and "amateur" recycling practices and fan inscription into the current model of media mix in the 1980s. For example, the Kadokawa "multimedia" company promoted popular novels like Yokomizô Seishi's detective stories though the simultaneous release of books, films, and original soundtracks.[18] But the first waves of media mix in otaku sanctuaries were also driven by informal exchanges between networks of acquaintances in retail shops and anime studios. These amateurish ventures can be seen as resembling the experimentations of fanzine and other independent markets.

More specifically, this tendency can be traced when looking at the early days of otaku mecca territories in Ikebukuro during the 1980s. Interviews of Inoue Shin'ichirô and Takahashi Yutaka, in particular, testify to the role of manga "bookstores" like Animate (1983), Manga no Mori (1989) or even Animepolispero (1980) in the diversification of anime paraphernalia and the ramifications of local networks of distribution. Although they started as "bookstores," most of these shops became more centered on anime paraphernalia in the 1990s and 2000s.[19] The case of Animate, previously called Lapôto, encapsulates some of the specificities of these (yet to be) official institutions: the former toy and pro-model retail shop abandoned Shinjuku and started selling manga-related paraphernalia near the Sunshine City Mall and the Toshimaoka School for girls. In other words, manga bookstores mobilized already existing media packets of moving images from books to small toys and school supplies. They also created new products on the local routes of cram schools and office buildings to satisfy a growing audience of schoolgirls and young working women. Another example of these local productions is the emergence of character songs and drama CDs, progressively invented in niche magazines, like *June*, and in stores, like Animate.

In this context, the thin barrier of male kinship between anime studios, manga publishers, and specialized retailers sustained the informal circulation of official celluloid, preparatory works *(settei)* and other illustrations; these were soon recycled by bookstores as postcards, posters, magazines, art books, and other paper-based media: "I went to Mushi Production and they gave me stuff that they were going to throw away."[20] Subsequently, recycling practices, even on the industrial level, started as a grey gift economy between former university or work acquaintances.

During this period,[21] as Kadokawa's editor Inoue recalls, manga and anime paraphernalia were rare commodities only distributed during short promotional events in department stores: "Buying character-goods was expensive because I had to take the train and half of my pocket-money was already gone."[22] The creation of bookstores specialized in the diversification of products was therefore a breakthrough in building translocal economies of "character goods" based on images specifically recycled by certain local stores. Each bookstore even used to produce their own catalogue-magazines expanding at times the circulation of their own "character goods" to mail orders. Animate's expansion from a local manga bookstore to a nationwide chain testifies to this legacy. Crucially, the project formulated by a large number of (male) otaku as an escape from a 9-to-5 office job by producing anime culture was concurrently met by the growing desire of female anime fans for new items, and it all continued to expand.[23]

At this point, I would like to briefly elaborate on the impact of the bookstore's milieu on "multimedia" practices as well as the progressive support provided by local institutions to fanzine production.[24] The aim is to delimit how the convergence of industrial and amateur recycling practices shaped both the evolution of sanctuaries territories and media-mix models. As such, the evolution of bookstores at the end of the 1980s highlight a progressive shift from multimedia adaptation strategies mostly represented by Kadokawa's entangled release of novels, films, and original soundtracks to Ôtsuka's concept of world-consumption theories. Developed in the late 1980s, this strategy incited fans to produce their own "episodes" by conceptualizing media connectivity through a specific "game" world. Resembling Propp's narrative theories, the parameters (settei) of a gamelike world could be reused by both the fans and the industry to produce more content feeding the same franchise. This strategy nonetheless understood the impact of the media complex of home TV: VHS, game, and live TV on otaku consumption but also the fan production of fanzines, OVA, and other texts as an important part of these niche markets. For instance, when explaining the birth of "light novels" (illustrated novels), Yamanaka described the role of niche "gaming" magazines to attract and recycle fan contents as official products while exploring new media commodities.[25]

However, the key role of the material dispersion of commodities in urban spaces as a tool to map consumers' networks represents one, often underestimated, element of Ôtsuka's world-consumption theory. As publishers like Kadokawa were hiring more and more otaku, they became particularly

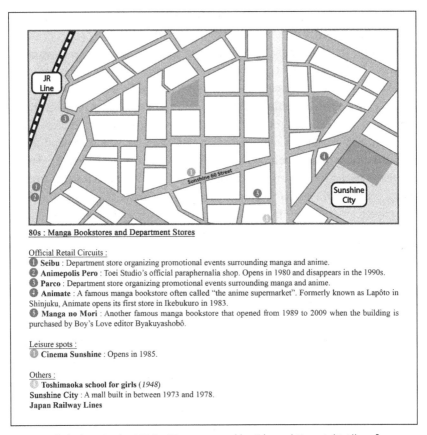

80s : Manga Bookstores and Department Stores

Official Retail Circuits :
1 **Seibu** : Department store organizing promotional events surrounding manga and anime.
2 **Animepolis Pero** : Toei Studio's official paraphernalia shop. Opens in 1980 and disappears in the 1990s.
3 **Parco** : Department store organizing promotional events surrounding manga and anime.
4 **Animate** : A famous manga bookstore often called "the anime supermarket". Formerly known as Lapôto in Shinjuku, Animate opens its first store in Ikebukuro in 1983.
5 **Manga no Mori** : Another famous manga bookstore that opened from 1989 to 2009 when the building is purchased by Boy's Love editor Byakuyashobô.

Leisure spots :
1 **Cinema Sunshine** : Opens in 1985.

Others :
Toshimaoka school for girls (*1948*)
Sunshine City : A mall built in between 1973 and 1978.
Japan Railway Lines

Figure 2. Ikebukuro in the 1980s. Map proposed by Edmond Ernest dit Alban from archival materials and interviews led in between 2015 and 2018. The '80s represent the original manga bookstore ecology, nearby schools, and railway stations.

sensitive to the urban distribution of niche markets. Because manga bookstores proposed all multimedia products like CDs, films, and novel products to be sold in the same shop, in the late 1980s and early 1990s, manga bookstores subsequently became the new bastion of media-mix strategies that had been originally divided between several institutions.[26] However, as the entanglement of multimedia production started to target niche magazines and niche shops, the status of local bookstores toward fanzine production also started to change. During this transition between the late 1980s and early 1990s, the growth of (mostly female) fanzine conventions and the emergence of fan made media recycling practices in otaku sanctuaries became evident when manga bookstores increasingly started to sell new and secondhand amateur manga and novels. This tendency intensified in the 1990s with the arrival in the neighborhood of bookstores becoming dedicated to secondhand fanzine and character goods, such as K-Books (1994, 1997, 1999), Toranoana (1996), and Mandarake (2004). The entangled relationship of the production of otaku media and otaku spaces is therefore revealed by the conjoined evolution of media mix and sanctuaries.

How, then, can we conceptualize the transformations of these first decades? Here it is important to consider how Ikebukuro's changes supported a shift in media-mix models: as Steinberg as well as Kawasaki and Ikura previously suggested, Kadokawa's media mix evolved from the mere diversification of products to the mobilization of fan participation.[27] Bookstores in the early 1990s mark the creation of fanzine "anthologies" (books reuniting various works from different artists) originally produced after conventions by associations between circles and small publishers; anthologies went on to become an industrial model for fan labor integration during the shift from multimedia to Ôtsuka's world-consumption theory.[28] With the economic context of the 1990s, "the paradise of fanzines" rapidly lost its economic independence, resulting in regular sponsorship (and control of fan content) from local bookstores, presses, and paraphernalia distributors.[29] The role of bookstores, as providers of both images and the tools to recycle them into fanzines, eventually evolved to a power structure that surveyed, policed, and capitalized on fan movements and production.

1990S–2000S: CHARACTER-MEDIA MIX, OTOME ROAD AND THE VERTICAL REGULATION OF WALKING AND RECYCLING INSIDE SANCTUARIES

It was in 2003 and I still remember it like it was yesterday. I had kept myself away from Yaoi for ten years. My office was next to the Takadanobaba station and I had to visit a client in Ikebukuro. I stumbled on a few fanzine shops like Aquahouse. K-Books just started to sell new fanzines for circles too (itaku) and I was amazed by the number of male-on-male romance manga and novels! I obviously immediately fell in the Yaoi-trap again. (Laughter).

—Pko, 46, journalist for a famous newspaper,
personal interview, June 2017

The divergences between the projects of space envisioned by fan and industrial recycling practices have recently become represented by the homoerotic female projects on the one hand and the newest media-mix strategy of the character-media mix on the other hand.[30] From the late 1990s to the early 2000s, the spatial and material convergence of fanzines with official goods in Tokyo's otaku sanctuaries started to (re)activate some tensions in the fan-industry relationship. With increasing concern for otaku "anime parody" pornography, and the aftermath of the infamous Pikachu and Tokimeki Memory controversies in 1999, fan recycling practices started to be more frequently questioned by worried mothers and publishers alike.[31] The grey gift economies of bookstores and anime studios moreover strictly transformed when facing the "disloyal" concurrence of fan made products. In other words, the incentive of world-consumption theories to integrate more fan narratives in official franchises failed to capture the exponential amateur production, leading to a progressive need to find new ways to tame them. As former convention organizer for Gamers (also known as Broccoli) Kidani testifies, it was indeed impossible for local institutions to produce more than fans: "Fanzines are just another form of 'character goods' (aka merchandise based on characters' images). People in the industry often ask why customers go to conventions like the Comiket but it is a rather simple issue; a thousand circles means a thousand different products. . . . As far as I know, if male fanzines are 'in danger' it is because of the rise of character goods. It's just like trading card games, there are too many of them!"[32]

While learning to imitate the rhythms, products, and spaces of female fan conventions converging in Ikebukuro, local institutions like Broccoli gradually displayed their need to institutionalize recycling practices and delimit the frontiers separating the official media mix from amateur, and ultimately, "fraud" products. In other words, world-consumption theory had to disappear in favor of media-mix strategies that regulated the too-large consumer, media, and content circulation. I would argue that the disappearance of numerous sponsored fanzine events in the nearby Sunshine City Mall after 1999, including the (in)famous Comic Castle, may represent signs of this deterioration of the relationship between the industry and fan production.[33] The progressive eradication of the practice of fan inclusion highlights a revision in the early 2000s of the position of fanzine and amateurship at the very bottom of the media-mix chain. Fundamentally, this (re)emergence of new media-mix practices focusing on characters and their official designs—a model also known as the "character-media mix"—coincides with the later acceleration of the tendencies ostracizing fanzines in the mid-2010s in Tokyo's sanctuaries.[34] Despite the stabilization of Otome Road around the secondhand economies of both amateur and industrial slash fiction made by women for women, local media-mix strategies tend to build a media ecology that limits the recycling of erotic male characters' images by fans.

Previous trends in Kadokawa's models also suggest similar developments. As famous characters such as Suzumiya Haruhi grew as their "own managers," the smaller windows for fan practices became even more limited. As an example, Steinberg explained how the dances in the Haruhi anime were one of the tools used to mobilize fan participation and to unify franchises as well as justify its unity across various media commodities.[35] The disappearance of the inclusion of fan creations inside text production then led to a radicalization of the event-based model in which limited edition products are made for a specific place, and a narrow schedule of distribution.[36] The current state of pedestrian transportation of character goods between official sites of distribution and secondhand recycle shops emerged from this spatial relationship between the industry and the fans. The only window left for fan reappropriation of media and content in the event media mix is the urban circulation of "used" media.

As such, the industrialization of female fanzines in the early 1990s represents a rather different example of fan labor integration than the character-media mix starting in the early 2000s; erotic and (non)pornographic slash manga's circulation in Ikebukuro reveals frequent slippery routes between the industry and fanzine conventions with many authors evolving in both spheres. The recognition of the homoerotic otaku feminine market with the institutionalization of Otome Road however allowed publishers and local retailers to progressively adapt the character-media mix strategy to the specific images of beautiful young boys *(bishônen)* of otaku women's fanzines in the mid-2000s.[37] In other words, the urban milieu of fragmented commodities envisioned by Ôtsuka—to make fans build worlds themselves—was replaced by carefully predetermined relations between media commodities forming routes between official retail stores. Ôtsuka wrote that there used to be no specific order between (official or amateur) media fragments but the one imagined by consumers. The character-media mix instrumentalized the limited circulation of characters' images to regulate the narrative possibilities of the series as well as pedestrian circulation.[38]

The evolution of secondhand shops and official retail stores around Otome Road testifies to the narrative, industrial, and spatial changes induced by this shift. Media circulating in Ikebukuro tended to focus less on narratives iterations of the series and more on accessories deriving from the official recycling of the character's official image and voice; the increase of accessories and audio stories (drama CDs) led to the creation of new recycle shops on Otome Road after 2005 (Figure 3). In the late 2000s and early 2010s, this situation also led to the current event-based media mix recycling the logics of local fan conventions and bookstores to lead consumers from a specific place to another in order to buy limited editions of randomized merchandise while limiting the grasp of fans on the reappropriation of character images.[39]

This tendency to drive consumers' transit in urban space but to also control their recycling practices nevertheless represents only one project of space in Ikebukuro. The case of the early emergence of Otome Road in the 2000s reveals the complex collision of two competing projects of spaces aiming at the same territories: the homoerotic manga routes and the character-media mix routes in between bookstores and merchandise retailers. Even before the crisis of the world-consumption theory, around 1992 female fanzines started to be integrated into the manga industry.[40] The production of amateur pornography in the Hardcore Yaoi fanzine in fact coexisted closely with the commercial magazines of Boys' Love and Lady Comics.[41]

Indeed, both Morikawa's and Sugiura's description of the origins of Otome Road as character good circulations and the space of male-on-male romance distribution reveal the merging of the local bookstore milieu with fanzines for female readers.[42] As described earlier, Ikebukuro's media recycling practices started in bookstores where fanzines were gradually (re)sold alongside character goods: K-books rapidly capitalized in the early 2000s on the massive production of both female fanzines and official goods. The occupation of local recycling networks by women also changed the originally male-oriented market of Ikebukuro through the combined forces of fanzines (including romantic, erotic, and pornographic ones), and manga occupying both "new" and secondhand local bookstores economies. Within the growing economy of slash books, secondhand bookstores like K-books, Mandarake, or KAQ shop thus officiated as centers of the production of feminine space in these sanctuaries.

But to what extent can we envision the invasion of the "acropolis of feminine fanzines" in Ikebukuro?[43] It is important to acknowledge that the media mix for women expanded around romance, erotic, and pornographic content made by women for women. For Misaki, producing media that was "satisfying themselves" and creating an alternative circuit of (mostly) pornographic circulation was fundamental to the construction of the women's route in Ikebukuro. When detailing the evolution of women's fanzine production and consumption Misaki described the progressive drift of an autonomous project

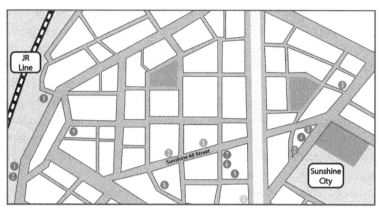

90s : Manga bookstores and second-hand stores

Official Retail Circuits :
❶ **Seibu** : Department store organizing promotional events surrounding manga and anime.
❷ **Animepolis Pero** : Toei Studio's official paraphernalia shop. Opens in 1980 and disappears in the 1990s.
❸ **Parco** : Department store organizing promotional events surrounding manga and anime.
❹ **Animate** : A famous manga bookstore often called "the anime supermarket". Formerly known as Lapôto in Shinjuku, Animate opens its first store in Ikebukuro in 1983.
❺ **Manga no Mori** : Another famous manga bookstore that opened from 1989 to 2009 when the building is purchased by Boy's Love editor Byakuyashobô.
❻ **Shinjuku-Shoten** : A bookstore with a rather famous space dedicated to fanzine. (1995 to the mid 2000s).
❼ **Gamers** : Anime merchandise company Broccoli's retail stores are mostly focused on video game paraphernalia (1996).
❽ **Toranoana** : A manga bookstore also selling fanzine (1998).
❾ **Tachibana-Shoten** : Yet another bookstore entangled in fanzine distribution (Opening and closing dates are unknown).

Leisure spots :
❶ **Sega Gigo**: Arcade (Game Center) (1993).
❷ **Cinema Sunshine** (*1985*)

Recycle shops and used Media :
❶ **K-Books** : Old books and "character goods" (anime and manga merchandise) (1994).
❷ **K-Books** : Old books and "character goods" (anime and manga merchandise) (1994, becomes the new Animate store in 2000).
❸ **K-Books** : Old fanzine (1997).

Others :
❶ **Toshimaoka school for girls** (*1948*)
Sunshine City : A mall built in between 1973 and 1978.
Japan Railway Lines

Figure 3. Ikebukuro in the 1990s. Map reconstructed by Edmond Ernest dit Alban from archival and ethnographic materials. The otaku geographies in the 1990s highlight a progressive invasion of the streets nearby the Sunshine City Mall by otaku recycling shops.

of space economically and symbolically independent from capitalist and consumerist values.[44] But, the integration of erotic and pornographic manga made by women for women to the larger industry seems to have helped the urban conquest of territories specific to female communities more than Misaki expected: "The promotional power of fanzines was always known. But it became harder to create Yaoi because the format of anthologies (book versions of fanzines) came too close to the original."[45] Ultimately, the growing support and control of certain institutions and publishers over fanzine production increased across the 1990s; Misaki's unease with the merging of industrial production with fanzines seems to have overlooked the massive urban impact of women's consumption and mobility.

Although female fanzines and manga still remain active as separate markets, their sustained exchanges produced pedestrian circuits of romance, erotic, and pornographic media (re)distribution available from convenience stores, to bookstores, specialized shops, recycling shops and fanzine conventions. In other words, the project to build a space for women by women held within feminine fanzines also established urban territories from its dialectics with industrial production. Their conjoined milieu gave visibility and renewed mobility for their publics. When Animate reopened in 2000, the entire store was designed to attract female consumers. K-books also expanded rapidly as both fancy butler cafés, and fanzine or character merchandise recycle shops. A few new fanzine shops (Aqua House, KAC shop) also opened in 2000 alongside general secondhand shops. The so-called maiden's road emerged because of the convergence of both amateur and official economies of recycled media and images.

In sum, urban sanctuaries like Ikebukuro emerged from the confrontations of multiple projects of space based on similar recycling practices, yet envisioned different regulations of urban circulation. As such, the entangled dialectics between feminine "pornography" and official (and "tamed") character's media mix continued to expand across the mid-2000s as both Boys' Love and character goods based on male characters simultaneously occupied the various local institutions. If the massive rise of recycle shops after the 2000s testifies to the conjoined expansion of both fanzine and character goods markets in the same territories, the recent evolution of Otome Road and its "dating simulation for girls" (Otome Games) nevertheless reveals a new conflict in the recycling of mostly 'beautiful boy' images and media. [46] The disputes mentioned in the introduction highlights how the "sexualized" bodies of male characters tend to be more and more prohibited in amateur forms, displacing the female fanzine to become an unofficial (and supposedly "dirty") practice. If the interdiction to produce amateur eroticopornographic fanzines of certain series is never really strictly applied, the right to dispose of (recycle) erotic images of sexy men and capitalize on their circulation therefore continues to draw lines between the projects of amateur and industrial communities.

The example of female fanzines in Otome Road and its integration into the manga industry nevertheless hints at a need for a mixed environment allowing the development and negotiations of multiple spaces and practices recycling mobile images. The history of Ikebukuro highlights how amateur and official media production cannot exist independently as they need each other to constantly evolve. This rapprochement of space and cultural production moreover illustrates Lefebvre's framework: media mix as a strategy to produce (or capture) pedestrian movement needs certain dialectics and alternative projects like fanzines to sustain its continuity. Fanzines, on the other hand, are often dependent on the industry to find new images to recycle. The convergence of multimedia products in bookstores, the failure of world-consumption theory to maintain otherness when merging fanzine and official production, and the emergence of the character-media mix to delimit the frontiers of official and fraud, might represent only a few of these dialectics of space reuniting the amateur and industrial projects of space.

Conclusion: Toward the Political Stakes of a Pedestrian History of Recycling Practices

Focusing on otaku recycling practices both on the levels of media production (reusing texts) and local secondhand economies (reselling media), I have tried to reveal the multiple actors of the conjoined histories of Otome Road in Ikebukuro (Tokyo) and media-mix strategies. Because local bookstores served as intermediaries between pedestrian communities and the industry, several official and amateur recycling practices spatially and materially converged to shape the actual landscape of the production of otaku space and media. But as Ikebukuro continues to be reimagined by local authorities as an important spot of official industrial manga and anime history, we must consider how consumer participation sustained this evolution.

The recent tendency of media-mix models to exclude amateur creations and police fan participation into "acceptable" consumption represents a hidden threat: while the industry's drive to control recycling practices only appears as an issue of regulating copyright infringement, the newly institutionalized

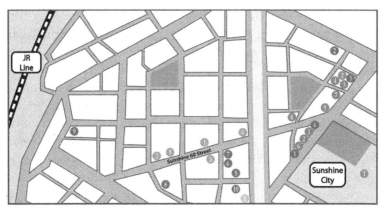

2000s : Otome-Road

Official Retail Circuits :

① **Animate** : The « anime supermarket » re-opens in 2000 directly on Otome-Road and is dedicated to feminine audiences.

② **KAC Shop** : Women's fanzine.

③ **Kingskings** : A "character goods" store opened by K-Books in 2004, this space will later become a recycle shop for women's fanzine in the late 2000s.

④ **Character Queen** : Opened in 2004, this "character goods" store is later purchased by K-Books in the late 2000s.

⑤ **Manga no Mori** : This manga bookstore existed until 2009, and then transformed by K-Books in 2011 into another recycle shop dedicated to musicals.

⑥ **Shinjuku-Shoten** : A manga bookstore, closed in 2005.

⑦ **Gamers** : Anime merchandise company Broccoli's retail stores are mostly focused on video game paraphernalia (1996).

⑧ **Toranoana** : A manga bookstore also selling fanzine (1998).

⑨ **Tachibana-Shoten** : Yet another bookstore entangled in fanzine distribution (Opening and closing dates are unknown).

⑩ **Anime Fantasia** : A "character goods" store closed in 2005.

Aquahouse : Out of the map in South Ikebukuro. Women's fanzine bookstore.

Leisure spots :

① **Sega Gigo**: Arcade (Game Center) (1993).

② **Adores** : Arcade (Game Center).

③ **DingDong** : Arcade (Game Center) (Became another Adores in 2012).

④ **St Tropez** : Arcade (Game Center).

⑤ **Cinema Sunshine** (*1985*)

Many Arcades open near Otome-Road in between the late 1990s and early 2000s. Arcades represent an often forgotten space for media mix and a source of inspiration for women's fanzine. Featuring fighting games, crane games and one coin toys, these institutions fed the second-hand economies of the sanctuary with images, contents and media to recycle.

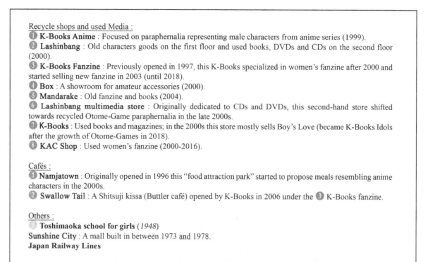

Recycle shops and used Media :
① **K-Books Anime** : Focused on paraphernalia representing male characters from anime series (1999).
② **Lashinbang** : Old characters goods on the first floor and used books, DVDs and CDs on the second floor (2000).
③ **K-Books Fanzine** : Previously opened in 1997, this K-Books specialized in women's fanzine after 2000 and started selling new fanzine in 2003 (until 2018).
④ **Box** : A showroom for amateur accessories (2000).
⑤ **Mandarake** : Old fanzine and books (2004).
⑥ **Lashinbang multimedia store** : Originally dedicated to CDs and DVDs, this second-hand store shifted towards recycled Otome-Game paraphernalia in the late 2000s.
⑦ **K-Books** : Used books and magazines; in the 2000s this store mostly sells Boy's Love (became K-Books Idols after the growth of Otome-Games in 2018).
⑧ **KAC Shop** : Used women's fanzine (2000-2016).

Cafés :
① **Namjatown** : Originally opened in 1996 this "food attraction park" started to propose meals resembling anime characters in the 2000s.
② **Swallow Tail** : A Shitsuji kissa (Buttler café) opened by K-Books in 2006 under the ③ K-Books fanzine.

Others :
⑨ **Toshimaoka school for girls** (*1948*)
Sunshine City : A mall built in between 1973 and 1978.
Japan Railway Lines

Figure 4. Ikebukuro in the 2000s. Map proposed by Edmond Ernest dit Alban from archival and ethnographic materials; some locations and dates may be questioned as many shops emerged and disappeared without leaving enough traces. The 2000s institutionalization of Otome Road significantly converges with the multiplication of official retail and recycle shops.

modes of event media mix also try to dictate how a fan can (or cannot) occupy urban space. For female fan communities, recycling represents a way for them to find their space, build networks, and construct a public sphere outside of the preexisting routes of circulation leading them to their house, to school, or to work. The otaku movement produces spaces for certain unstable niche groups to emerge and their efforts are entangled with the official industry. The transformations of sanctuaries like Otome Road reveals the commonplace negotiation between theses marginal social groups—or at least groups put in a marginal position—and industrial power structures.

The increasing popularity of sanctuaries, I would argue, highlights a need for alternative rhythms in everyday life. Placed on the way back home from school and work, Otome Road represents a space for daily breaks for exhausted women. When looking at the early 2000s, most of the media production of Ikebukuro was also produced by women for women, from Ruby Party's video games to slash manga and novels. As such, we could question the impact of these nonsedentary pedestrian female communities searching for their own place in urban space as the invention of a temporary form of (literal) "citizenship," as being a part of the city, a transient strategy of capture, and an unstable, yet repetitive, mode of sociopolitical accountability based on techniques of recycling mobile images. Recycling logics gives infrapolitical communities the tools to invent themselves through the production of specific modes of expressions circulating in delimited urban territories.[47]

In other words, the case of otaku sanctuaries reveals how the entangled production of otaku space and media through the dissemination of moving images represents a political phenomenon we (academics) need to address: Azuma Sonoko recently reminded us of this matter when describing the female fanzine as a tool to invade public space and rebuild a feminine public intimacy.[48] The focus on the recovery of women's agency in the study of women's slash manga could subsequently extend to their spatial agency built with the recycling of these media in Ikebukuro. When recycling images to produce their own media and recycling media to produce their own space, pedestrian women shaped the successive models of media mix. As their project of space became evident with the settling of Otome Road, women were recognized as a market, as an ensemble of niche audiences, and as citizens participating in local, regional, and national cultural politics. Fan agency is evolving from a consumer one to a citizen-like position and this transformation should be further explored.

Edmond Ernest dit Alban is a cotutelle PhD candidate at Concordia University (Cinema Studies) and Paris Saint Denis University (Communication Studies). His dissertation examines a pedestrian approach to the Japanese popular otaku culture in Ikebukuro (Tokyo) by focusing on girl fanzine and paraphernalia circulation. His publications include a research report for the online journal *gamenvironments*, a forthcoming article analyzing the evolution of urban marketing for women in Japan for *Synoptique,* and a chapter co-written with Marc Steinberg for Paul Booth's *Companion to Media and Fandom Studies: Otaku Pedestrians* (2018).

Notes

1. Marc Steinberg and Edmond Ernest dit Alban, "Otaku Pedestrians," *A Companion to Media Fandom and Fan Studies,* ed. Paul Booth (Hoboken: Wiley-Blackwell, 2018), 289–304.

2. Marc Steinberg, *Anime's Media Mix: Franchising Toys and Characters in Japan* (Minneapolis: University of Minnesota Press, 2012), xi; Marc Steinberg, *Naze nihon ha media mix suru kuni nanoka* (Tokyo: Kadokawa, 2015), 7–9.

3. Thomas Lamarre, *The Anime Machine* (Minneapolis: University of Minnesota Press, 2009), xvi; Thomas Lamarre, "Introduction to Otaku Movement," *EnterText* 4, no. 1 (Winter 2004/2005): 151–87.

4. Thomas Lamarre, *The Anime Ecology* (Minneapolis: University of Minnesota Press, 2018), 111–20; Henry Lefebvre, *La production de l'espace* (Paris: Persée, 1974), 53.

5. Azuma Sonoko, *Takarazuka Yaoi: Ai no yomikae josei to popyûrakaruchâ no shakaigaku* (Takarazuka Yaoi: The double reading of love: A sociology of women and popular culture) (Tokyo: Shinyôsha, 2015), 241.

6. Patrick W. Galbraith and Christodoulou Androniki, *Otaku Spaces* (Seattle: Chin Music Press: 2012); Morikawa Ka'ichirô, *Shûto no tanjô* (The birth of the hobby city) (Tokyo: Genshôsha, 2003), 42.

7. Kawasaki Takuhito and Iikura Yoshiyuki, "Ranobe kyara ha tachôsakuhin sekai no yume wo miruka" (Are characters dreaming of multiple worlds?), in *Raitonoberu kenkyûjosetsu* (An introduction to light novel studies), ed. Ichiyanagi and Kume, 18–32 (Tokyo: Seikyûsha, 2009).

8. Anne McKnight, "Frenchness and the Transformation of Japanese Subculture, 1972–2004," *Mechademia* 5 (Minneapolis: University of Minnesota Press, 2010), 118–37; Ôtsuka Eiji, *Otaku no seishin: 1980 nendai ron* (Otaku's mind: Debating about the 1980s) (Tokyo: Seikaisha, 2016), 5–30.

9. Okamoto Takeshi, *Nijisôsaku kankô (Content Tourism)* (Hokkaidô: Ebetsu, 2012), 50–51; *Seichi junrei: Sekaiisan kara anime no butai made* (Pilgrimage: From world heritage to anime scenes) (Tokyo: Chûkôshinsho, 2015), 53–55.

10. Steinberg and Ernest dit Alban, "Otaku Pedestrians," 293.

11. Tanaka Ema, "Industrial Structure of 'Japan Cool': Co-existence of Media-mix and Diversity of Contents by Production Commission Systems in Japan," *The Journal of the Japan Association for Social and Economic Systems Studies* 30 (2009): 45–53.

12. Sugiura Yumiko, *Otaku joshi kenkyû: Fûjoshi shisô taikei* (A study of girl otaku: The case of fûjoshi imagination) (Tokyo: Harashobo, 2006), 16; Morikawa Ka'ichirô, "Higashi Ikebukuro ni Otome Road ha naze shutsugen shita no ka" (Why did otome road emerged in east Ikebukuro?), *Comiket catalogue 68* (2005), retrieved from http://www.kyoshin.net/aide/c68_1/07.html.

13. Ôtsuka Eiji, "Kadokawashoten no hadakankaku to animeito no tetsugaku," *Neppu sutajio jiburi no kôkishin* 9, no. 12 (Tokyo: Studio Ghibli, 2011): 31–48; AIDE, "Higashi ikebukuro senmonten no shûchû," *Comiket catalogue 68*, retrieved from http://www.kyoshin.net/aide/c68_1/08.html.

14. Okada Toshio, *Otakugakunyûmon* (An introduction to otakuology) (Tokyo: Futada, 1996); Nishimura Mari, *Yaoi to Aniparo* (Tokyo: Futada, 2002), 20.

15. Yoda Tomiko, "Girlscape: The Marketing of Mediatic Ambience in Japan," *Media Theory in Japan*, ed. Alexander Zhalten and Marc Steinberg, 173-99 (Durkham: Duke University Press, 2017).

16. Lamarre, *The Anime Machine*, 16-18; Ian Condry, The Soul of Anime: Collaborative Creativity and Japan's Media Success Story (Durham: Duke University Press, 2013), 70-71; Steinberg, *Anime's Media Mix*, 16.

17. Nishi Mari, *Aniparo to yaoi* (Anime parody and yaoi) (Tokyo: Futada, 2001), 18-45.

18. Alexander Zahlten, *The End of Japanese Cinema: Industrial Genres, National Times and Media Ecologies* (Durham: Duke University Press, 2017), 122-25.

19. Ôtsuka, "Kadokawashoten no hadakankaku," 31-48.

20. Ôtsuka, "Kadokawashoten no hadakankaku," 31-48.

21. Ôtsuka Eiji, *Teihon monogatari shôhiron* (A theory of book consumption) (Tokyo: Kadokawa, 2001), 7-20.

22. Ôtsuka, "Kadokawashoten no hadakankaku," 31-48.

23. Ôtsuka, *Otaku no seishin*, 23-27; Shannon Kinsella, *Adult Manga: Culture and Power in Contemporary Japan* (Honolulu: University of Hawaii Press, 2000), 102-38.

24. Zahlten, *The End of Japanese Cinema*, 122-25; Kawasaki and Iikura, "Ranobe kyara ha tachôsakuhin," 18-32.

25. Yamanaka Tomomi, "Raitonoberushi saikô" (Revisiting light novel history), in *Raitonoberusutadîzu* (Light novel studies), ed. Ichiyanagi and Kume (Tokyo: Seikyûsha, 2013).

26. Yoda, "Girlscape," 173-99.

27. Marc Steinberg, "Media Mix Mobilization: Social Mobilization and Yo-kai Watch," *Animation*, 12, no. 3 (Sage, 2017): 244-58; Kawasaki and Iikura, "Ranobe kyara ha tachôsakuhin," 18-32.

28. Misaki Naoto, *Shôjotachi ha rakuen wo mezasu* (Girls heading to heaven), (self-published, 1990), retrieved from http://www.st.rim.or.jp/~nmisaki/works2/rakuen.html; Misaki Naoto, *Shôgyôansorojii to okosamatachi: Gakeppuchi de sukippu suru ojôsamatachi* (Commercial anthologies and children: Young girls a step ahead the cliff), (self-published, 1996), retrieved from http://www.st.rim.or.jp/~nmisaki/works2/repo_book.html#FLAG7.

29. Misaki, *Shôgyôansorojii to okosamatachi.*

30. Lefebvre, *La production de l'espace,* 53.

31. Anne Allison, *Permitted and Prohibited Desires: Mothers, Comics and Censorship in Japan* (University of California Press, 1996); Nagayama Kaoru, *Sôho ero manga sutadiizu: Kairaku sôchi toshite no manga nyûmon* (Expended ero manga studies: An introduction to manga as a device for pleasure) (Tokyo: Chikuma, 2014), 99–119; Miyamoto Naoki, *Eroge bunka kenkyûgairon* (Eroge cultural studies) (Tokyo: sôgôkagaku, 2012), 90.

32. "Tokushû kigyô tanken intabyû: Ibento kaisaisha ni kiku dôjinshi sokubaikai komikkukyassuru ga owaru," (Special interview of the industry: We asked to an event company about the end of the Comic Castle convention), *Aide Shinbun* 36 (May 3, 1998), retrieved from http://www.kyoshin.net/aide/a36/04.html.

33. "Tokushû kigyô tanken intabyû."

34. Steinberg, *Naze nihon ha media mix suru kuni nanoka,* 255–73.

35. Steinberg, *Naze nihon ha media mix suru kuni nanoka,* 255–73.

36. Steinberg and Ernest dit Alban, "Otaku Pedestrians," 293.

37. Mori Naoko, *Onna ha poruno wo yomu josei to seiyoku to feminizumu* (Women read porn: Women and sexual desire and feminism) (Tokyo: Seikyusha, 2010).

38. Ôtsuka, *Teihon monogatari shôhiron,* 235.

39. Steinberg and Ernest dit Alban, "Otaku Pedestrians," 289–304.

40. Azuma, *Takarazuka Yaoi,* 153.

41. Mori, *Onna ha poruno,* chap. 2.

42. Morikawa, "Higashi Ikebukuro ni Otome Road"; Sugiura, *Otaku joshi kenkyû,* 16.

43. Kaneda Junko, "Manga dôjinshi: Kaishakukyôdôtai no poritikusu," (Manga fanzine: the politics of common readings), *Bunka no shakaigaku* (Cultural sociology), ed. Sato and Yoshimi, 163–90 (Tokyo: Yuhikaku, 2007).

44. Misaki, *Shôjotachi ha rakuen wo mezasu*; Misaki, *Shôgyôansorojii to okosamatachi.*

45. Misaki, *Shôgyôansorojii to okosamatachi.*

46. Koide Chitoko and Obana Takashi, "Historical Analysis of Otome Games: Focus on the Character Analysis," *Research Bulletin of Osaka Shoin Women's University* 8 (Kobe: Shoin University, 2018), 69–74.

47. James C. Scott, *The Moral Economy of the Peasant: Rebellion and Subsistence in South East Asia* (New Haven: Yale University Press, 1979).

48. Azuma, *Takarazuka Yaoi,* 211–42.

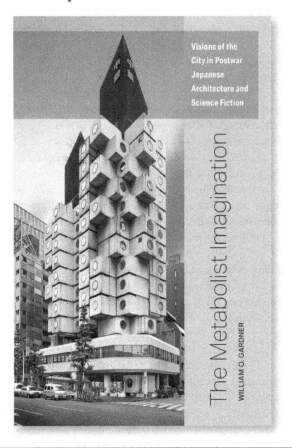